W9-DBE-359

Regis College Library
15 ST. MARY STREET
TORONTO, ONTARIO, CANADA
M4Y 2R5

CONCILIUM

Religion in the Eighties

CONCILIUM

Editorial Directors

Giuseppe Alberigo	Bologna	Italy
Gregory Baum	Montreal	Canada
Willem Beuken SJ	Nijmegen	The Netherlands
Leonardo Boff	Petrópolis	Brazil
Paul Brand	Ankeveen	The Netherlands
Antoine van den Boogaard	Nijmegen	The Netherlands
Ann Carr	Chicago, Ill.	USA
Marie-Dominique Chenu OP	Paris	France
Julia Ching	Toronto	Canada
John Coleman SJ	Berkeley, Ca.	USA
Mary Collins OSB	Wake Forest, NC	USA
Yves Congar OP	Paris	France
Christian Duquoc OP	Lyons	France
Virgil Elizondo	San Antonio, Texas	USA
Casiano Floristán	Madrid	Spain
Sean Freyne	Dublin	Ireland
Claude Geffré OP	Paris	France
Norbert Greinacher	Tübingen	West Germany
Gustavo Gutiérrez	Lima	Peru
Herman Häring	Nijmegen	The Netherlands
Bas van Iersel SMM	Nijmegen	The Netherlands
Jean-Pierre Jossua OP	Paris	France
Hans Küng	Tübingen	West Germany
Nicholas Lash	Cambridge	Great Britain
Mary Mananzan OSB	Manila	Philippines
Norbert Mette	Münster	West Germany
Johann-Baptist Metz	Münster	West Germany
Dietmar Mieth	Tübingen	West Germany
Jürgen Moltmann	Tübingen	West Germany
Alphonse Ngindu Mushete	Kinshasa	Zaire
Aloysius Pieris SJ	Gonawala-Kelaniya	Sri Lanka
Jacques Pohier	Paris	France
David Power OMI	Washington, DC	USA
James Provost	Washington, DC	USA
Karl Rahner SJ +	Innsbruck	Austria
Giuseppe Ruggieri	Catania	Italy
Edward Schillebeeckx OP	Nijmegen	The Netherlands
Elisabeth Schüssler Fiorenza	Cambridge, Ma.	USA
David Tracy	Chicago, Ill.	USA
Knut Walf	Nijmegen	The Netherlands
Anton Weiler	Nijmegen	The Netherlands
Christos Yannaras	Athens	Greece

General Secretariat: Prins Bernhardstraat 2, 6521 AB Nijmegen, The Netherlands

Concilium 200 (6/1988): Exegesis/Church History

CONCILIUM

List of Members

Advisory Committee: Exegesis/Church History

Directors:

Wim Beuken SJ	Nijmegen	The Netherlands
Sean Freyne	Dublin	Ireland

Members:

Luis Alonso Schökel SJ	Rome	Italy
John Ashton	Oxford	Great Britain
Hans Barstad	Oslo	Norway
Germain Bienaimé	Tournai	Belgium
Brendan Byrne SJ	Parkville/Vict.	Australia
Antony Campbell SJ	Parkville/Vict.	Australia
J. Cheryl Exum	Chestnut Hill/Ma.	USA
Aelred Cody OSB	St. Meinrad/Ind.	USA
Vicente Collado Bertomeu	Valencia	Spain
José Severino Croatto CM	Buenos Aires	Argentina
Lucas Grollenberg OP	Nijmegen	The Netherlands
Herbert Haag	Lucerne	Switzerland
Bas van Iersel SMM	Nijmegen	The Netherlands
Hans-Winfried Jüngling SJ	Frankfurt/Main	West Germany
Othmar Keel	Freiburg	Switzerland
Hans-Josef Klauck	Würzburg	West Germany
Jonathan Magonet	London	Great Britain
Sean McEvenue	Montreal/Quebec	Canada
Martin McNamara MSC	Blackrock/Co. Dublin	Ireland
Halvor Moxnes	Oslo	Norway
Roland Murphy OCarm	Durham/NC	USA
Robert Murray SJ	London	Great Britain
Magnus Ottosson	Uppsala	Sweden
Elisabeth Pascal-Gerlinger	Strasbourg	France
John Riches	Glasgow	Great Britain
Elisabeth Schüssler Fiorenza	Cambridge/Ma.	USA
Angelo Tosato	Rome	Italy
Marc Vervenne	Louvain	Belgium
Adela Yarbro Collins	Notre Dame/Ind.	USA

TRUTH AND ITS VICTIMS

Edited by
Wim Beuken
Sean Freyne
and
Anton Weiler

English Language Editor
James Aitken Gardiner

Regis College Library
15 ST. MARY STREET
TORONTO, ONTARIO, CANADA
M4Y 2R5

WITHDRAWN

96297

BT
10
C64
v. 200

T. & T. CLARK LTD
Edinburgh

Copyright © 1988, by Stichting Concilium and T. & T. Clark Ltd
All rights reserved. No part of this publication shall be reproduced, stored in a retrieval
system, or transmitted, in any form or by any means, electronic, mechanical,
photocopying, rewording or otherwise, without the written permission of Stichting
Concilium, Prins Bernhardstraat 2, 6521 AB Nijmegen, Holland; and T. & T. Clark
Ltd, 59 George Street, Edinburgh, Scotland, EH2 2LQ.

December 1988
ISBN: 0 567 30080 3

ISSN: 0010-5236

Typeset by C. R. Barber & Partners (Highlands) Ltd, Fort William
Printed by Page Brothers (Norwich) Ltd

Concilium: Published February, April, June, August, October, December.
Subscriptions 1988: UK: £27.50 (including postage and packing); USA: US$49.95
(including air mail postage and packing); Canada: Canadian$59.95 (including air mail
postage and packing); other countries: £27.50 (including postage and packing).

CONTENTS

Part III
Church History: Opponents from Within and Without

Part IV
Concluding Article

CONCILIUM 200 Special Column

James Provost and Knut Walf

The Selection of Bishops

NOT A question of dogma, nor a mystery necessary for salvation, nor an essential to one's faith in God, the issue of how their bishop is selected still raises more passion in dioceses awaiting a new chief pastor. Even to address this issue raises more emotion among certain church authorities.

Why this emotional response? It may be a validation of the Second Vatican Council's teaching on the importance of bishops. But it may also be the sign of growing danger, a danger which is viewed differently along the Tiber from other places in the world.

There is no divinely revealed manner for selecting successors in the episcopal college. If there were, open nomination within the community and selection by casting lots would be needed for valid selection of bishops (cf. Acts 1:15–26). Historically there have been many ways in which leaders of local churches have been selected. This is not to claim any one of them is perfect, or must be preserved at all costs. It is to state, however, that the present system is as open to the judgment of history—and to criticism of its viability—as any other system of selecting bishops.

On what basis should a system for selection of bishops be judged? Is it that it is carried out according to the law? Or that it is in keeping with historical developments of central authority? Or that it promotes the unity of faith and the preaching of the Gospel, the spiritual purpose of ministry and the common good of the Church?

This latter basis, espoused by the highest authorities in the Church, is not an abstract judgment. The adequacy, or inadequacy, of a given system for selecting bishops can be judged depending on whether the unity of the Church is indeed promoted, or whether it is hindered by the system—depending on whether the Gospel is truly preached in a way accommodated to the needs of the listeners and the needs of the times, or not. The system of selecting bishops will be judged, then, on whether the

xiii

spiritual purpose of ministry does indeed shine through, and whether the common good of the Church is evidently promoted.

Recent events raise serious questions about the adequacy of the present system. Major dioceses on many continents have been left vacant for long periods of time. Bishops who have submitted their resignation at the age of 75 must wait one or even two years for a response. In some cases, bishops are selected who clearly lack the basic capacity for leadership.

Moreover, far from protecting the Church from the formation of pressure groups or 'parties', the current system actually fosters them. The secrecy of the system, its limitation to a select group of 'powerful figures', its lack of open accountability, produces a climate in which political pressures and special interests can have free rein.

It is also a system in which the operative criteria for selecting bishops remains hidden, despite statements of pastoral and spiritual beauty. Is loyalty to certain disciplinary norms more important than effectiveness in preaching the Gospel? Is adherence to a particular movement, mentality, or political persuasion more important than ability to foster the life of the Christian community? The evidence is mixed, and for that very reason makes it all the more difficult to justify the current system which is so centralised, secretive, and open to influence peddling.

Indeed, the present system is far from the practice of the first centuries of the Church, and from the principle of relative ordination then in force. In a system in which only the pope makes the selection the Church becomes more and more removed from its origins. Is this not an ecclesiological, theological problem? Does it not pose serious ecumenical questions?

This is not a plea to 'democratise' the selection of bishops, nor to deny the proper role of the petrine ministry in the communion of churches. It is, however, a patient request that the process for selecting bishops be weighed, not for its short-term benefits, but for its long-term results. Is the long-term good of the Church not to be found in developing strong local churches, aware of their responsibility within the communion of churches and confident of their leadership?

We do not offer a new system, much less a 'perfect' system, for selecting bishops. But we do propose that the issue of how bishops are selected needs a fresh examination throughout the Church. Do not the spiritual purpose of the ministry and the common good of the Church require at least this much?

Note that this Special Column, like others in this series, is written under the sole responsibility of the authors.

TRUTH AND ITS VICTIMS

Editorial

OUR TITLE is deliberately paradoxical, especially for Christians who believe with St John that 'the truth will make you free' (John 7:32). Sadly, however, there are many victims strewn across the pages of history who have been victimised in the name of the truth to which the Christian Church feels called on to witness. Christian consciousness of that history has been heightened in the present century not only by events such as the holocaust, but also by the growing awareness of the ideology of patriarchy and the massive exploitation of the poor, which both feminist and liberation theology continue to draw to our attention. These concerns are never far from the pages of *Concilium*, and in this issue also, we seek to address them, somewhat more obliquely, perhaps, by recognising the need to approach even our classical, sacred texts and our history in a critical fashion.

Christians must always live in the present while remembering the past and striving to fashion a future which is in greater conformity with the truth of God's universal care and concern disclosed in Jesus Christ. Our theological task is, then, to appropriate that past critically, without allowing it to function as an ideology which can dominate any or all of those who, in whatever way, perceive themselves as victims in our world and are in search of a genuinely liberative truth. Thus, there are two horizons which must constantly be kept in tension, namely, our own as interpreters in search of such a liberative truth and that of those texts which continue to demand our attention, but which we know, are themselves often the product of conflicting points of view, and have their own hidden ideologies at work.

The historical-critical method, with the increasing aid of the social sciences in the study of the Bible and the emphasis on social and cultural history in the investigation of later Christian theology, has achieved a much greater awareness of the conditioning of our texts and has helped to expose the hidden ideologies lurking within the most innocent accounts of our sacred past. It is this horizon which in the main the current issue attempts to address, while also keeping in mind that we are in constant danger of repressing or misrepresenting it and that we must listen carefully to the ways in which the victims in our own world read the past. Acknowledging that there never was a 'golden age' in which there were no victims or victors in human affairs, we wish to ask our sacred record—Jewish and Christian—how in fact it has regarded its victims: as objects of God's universal care or as chattels to be abandoned to the scrap heap of history? In our search for a genuinely liberative praxis for our own world in which the dualism of victors and vanquished might be transcended, we wish to address the ambiguities of the past both honestly and critically, recognising that in many and hidden ways these contribute to our own ideological biases, precisely because we have received them as authoritative within our tradition.

The Old Testament contributions examine the ways in which historiography and prophecy have sought to emphasise Israel's duty to protect potential victims of its own triumph and of the ideological abuse of the promise to David, both of which were given by God, and were not, therefore, Israel's achievement by which it might dominate others.

The remembrance of the Egyptian slavery in the Book of Exodus and its impact on the legislation concerning the treatment of slaves and other vulnerable groups, functions, according to Jonathan Magonet, as an 'anti-model' for the society Israel was to create. In this way it was, he claims, shielded, from triumphalistic feelings that would serve its own interests.

It is well-known that Scripture has assessed the Davidic-Solomonic kingdom as religiously ambiguous. Hans Winfried Jüngling examines this phenomenon in two exemplary texts: the scandalous story of David and Bathsheba (2 Sam. 11–12) and the political confrontation between Isaiah and Ahaz (Isa. 7). The presentation of the tyrannic king who does not eschew assassination, has as background the royal ideology, according to which the king is the warrant of justice and care for the poor (Ps. 72). Since the kingdom derives its sacral character from God it was never considered absolute in the sense of being free to ignore standards of faith and ethics—not even in the political realm.

Israel's attitude to the nations is a third topic. As Bernard Renaud demonstrates, the prophetic movement is responsible for the view that Israel's history will not be written as the power story of a national god who vindicates his people against the peoples of other gods, but as the story of an ethical appeal that applies to Israel as well as to the nations. This fundamental prophetic conception developed in three stages: the break-up of the nationalistic horizon (Amos 1–2); the way of conversion becoming open to the other nations also (Jonah); the calling of the nations to the community of the covenant (Isa. 19:16–25).

The three New Testament contributions continue this questioning of the past. How have Christians reacted to the status of victims—religiously from the synagogue, towards dissidents within its own ranks and politically, under Rome?

Matthew's gospel provides an interesting sounding board for Christian attitudes towards Jews, according to Sean Freyne. In this 'most Jewish' of early Christian writings, we hear a Christian scribe/evangelist seeking to establish the claims of his own community at the expense of other Jewish groups by a combination of Greco-Roman and apocalyptic vituperative rhetoric. This reading of the text provokes the question: how can we avoid allowing our claims to truth becoming the ideology that enslaves others?

The first Epistle of John, with its sublime declaration 'God is love' also points to a community deeply divided on the truth of the Gospel. Hans-Josef Klauck examines the author's inability to resolve the tension—so rarely dealt with satisfactorily in Christian history—of combining a concern for the correct understanding of faith with the principle of universal love, without reducing it into a formless 'love concern' that abandons its distinctively Christian content.

Of all the New Testament writings the Book of Revelation—with its unrestrained symbolism the product of a highly creative Christian imagination—is most open to ideological abuse. The articles of Adela Yarbro Collins and Christopher Rowlands approach this book with the two horizons already outlined—that of the texts and that of victims in our own world—broadly in view. The former reads the book from the perspective of how the oppressor, Rome, is viewed, paying careful attention to its negative symbolisation and to its use of violent language to predict its destruction. The stance of the author may be elucidated, both on psychological and sociological grounds, it is suggested, given the tension between faith and the experience of oppression. Yet the response—violent images, for example, rather than violent action—is at best unstable and imperfect and raises the question of what does it profit 'the oppressed to become oppressors'.

By way of contrast to this careful attention to the rhetoric of the text in relation to its original circumstances, Rowlands approaches the book from a radical Christian perspective today. He sees it as the keeping alive of a messianic ideal which early Christianity inherited from Judaism, with its dangerous memory for the rich and powerful and its release of energy for social change. As such it differs from those other early literary expressions of the new movement, such as the letter form, which stress continuity with the existing social order, and do not, therefore, have within them the same social dynamic that the book of Revelation has.

This contrast of approaches to a particular book serves to remind us of the need for a pluralism of readings if we are to do full justice to the horizons both of the text and the modern world. The more historically orientated reading avoids any idealisation of the text by pointing to the ambiguities in the author's point of view, while an interpretative stance that is located within a modern critical faith-perspective shows how a text with such internal ambiguity—and therefore, such potentiality for supporting a sectarian point of view—can still function critically when the interpreter's own position is pre-determined by the Gospel demands of peace and justice.

The Editorial Board had planned a number of different contributions for the historical section of this issue of *Concilium*. For instance, we thought of including something on the treatment of gnosticism by the ascendant orthodox Church, and of an article on the way in which the Church dealt with Arius and his adherents. We also considered as a subject the treatment by the Church of England of nonconformists and dissenters. The violent aspects of the whole area of orthodoxy and heterodoxy comprise an all too well substantiated part of the history of the Church. Unfortunately, in the end these articles could not be provided. Nevertheless, the contributions which we have been able to offer in this *Concilium* converge in an interesting way.

Gonnet discusses the position of Cathars and Waldensians in the bosom of the mediaeval Church as a model of the treatment of opponents within a church community. Reformers' zeal, scriptural and spiritual radicalism, gnostic tendencies and popular evangelism are various strands in the construction of a new ecclesiology. The need to reform the Church inside and out often drew pressure from the opposition within the Church, and harsh repression in the shape of inquisitions and crusades. Honée describes how the Lutherans reacted to the sixteenth-century Anabaptists, and shows how the Church attitude to the Anabaptists is also associated with its attitude to the régime. Ought we to identify the Church and Christendom? We must not forget that differences of opinion on such matters often resulted in downright persecution.

Reeves stresses the fact in the thirteenth century the essential question was one of how the saints live and who is the antichrist. Franciscan spiritual writers identified outsiders externally as the antichrist, but the official Church in its turn expelled the spiritual pundits and their followers from the Church as radicals. Hostile images played a major part in this kind of spiritual offensive. But the Bible and theology were also mobilised in the campaign against the 'others'. Weiler studies the question concerning how the doctrine of a holy—i.e. justified—war produced theological arguments which allowed the trouncing of 'outsiders' in the name of God. Erbe shows how in the actual case of Charlemagne's conquest of Saxony there was an interesting intermingling of missionary and political submission. Initially, the Saxons saw the acceptance of Christianity as the only way of maintaining their political independence, but submission and repression arrived along with missionary activity. Dussel reveals the rhetoric of the traditional western mode of historical writing, which talks of the 'discovery' of America when the continent had already been inhabited by human beings for a very long time. The image of the oppressed and their destiny up to the twentieth century reveals the reconceptualisation of historical studies, which in the tracks of Hegel identified western Christianity with civilisation. The history of Christianity and colonisation in Africa in the nineteenth and twentieth centuries, as described by Obdeijn, shows some striking parallels with the findings of Erbe and Dussel.

In a concluding article that serves to make explicit the horizon of modern victims, Ottmar John makes a plea for the privileged position of the poor, who, as victims of history are open to a radical message of liberation as gift. Essentially, this is the message of the Gospel, of which our history must be the bearer, but which it has in fact often sadly distorted. According to John the poor relate to the past differently from those who operate from a position of social and economic dominance. These either exploit the past in order to underpin their own power, or alternatively, ignore it as irrelevant in a modern world which emphasises human achievements as being self-produced and totally independent of history. This role of privileged readers which he wishes to attribute to the poor is not, according to John, a given of their condition, but is only theirs if they recognise that condition as a call to resist in faith, hope and love the causes of their oppression.

It is then by seeking to do the truth in love, while at the same time being critically aware of the dark side of every human success in terms of others being at least potential victims, that we may—hopefully—avoid some of the tragedies of our Christian history, which this number of *Concilium* has sought to expose.

Wim Beuken
Sean Freyne
Anton Weiler

PART I

Old Testament

Jonathan Magonet

The Attitude Towards Egypt in the Book of Exodus

IT WOULD be hard to overestimate the importance of Egypt in Israelite consciousness for the Bible writers. The story of the exodus, as well as being central to the Israelite understanding of their origins, becomes a model for interpreting the Babylonian exile and the return. The remembrance of Egyptian slavery becomes a crucial concept underlying the legislation concerned not only with the treatment of slaves, but of all resident aliens and all vulnerable social groups. The later history of the two kingdoms is intimately bound up with the political vicissitudes of the regional 'superpowers'. Though alliances with Egypt were attacked by the prophets, this antagonism relates to a distrust of any such political dependencies and a scepticism about the reliability of Egypt as an ally. There is almost none of the anger and hatred that sometimes characterise the views of Assyria and Babylon. The memory and depiction of Egypt is thus surprisingly sympathetic despite it being the 'house of slaves' from which they saw themselves as having emerged.

The book of Exodus is either a source of this attitude or a reflection of it, depending on one's view of the historical development of these texts.

The first section of the book tells a story. In its overview and in its details it transmits to later generations a particular perception of the experience of Egypt. The repeated instructions to teach your children about the events of the exodus (Exod. 10:2; 12:26; 13:8, 14), which will subsequently lie at the heart of the elaborate Jewish Passover Seder, reinforce the feeling that each detail of what happened is enormously significant. The exodus events are

11

important in broad theological terms (God's intervention in human history and concern with the fate of His people) and in terms of the set of human values they instill (freedom from slavery, 'liberation'). But in the first instance the story portrays the political negotiations between Pharaoh and Moses and it is these that we must examine.

1. 'HEROES' AND 'VILLAINS'

It is vital to notice from the outset that the Egyptians are not depicted as uniformly wicked, nor, for that matter, are the Israelites all good, or, at least, instantly faithful to their God. A Pharaoh is the instigator of events and his successor continues his policies, but his officers and the Egyptian people in general are represented as distinct from him and finally in opposition to his actions. It is that sort of discrimination that must be borne in mind when evaluating the overall view of Egypt.

The story begins with the dramatic announcement of the 'arising' of a new king over Egypt who did not know Joseph. The use of the terminology of 'a new king' has long suggested the possibility that this marked a dynastic change. In such a situation the wider implications of the terminology of 'knowing' or 'not knowing' Joseph become clearer—the refusal to 'acknowledge' the power or position or legitimacy of an appointee of the previous regime and his successors. This sense of the word is reinforced when we follow the use of this same hebrew verb *yada* throughout this section. Not only does Pharaoh not 'know' Joseph, his successor will not *know* the God of the Hebrews (Exodus 5:2) and part of the intention of the plagues will be the frequently stated purpose to make sure that Pharaoh and the Egyptians do come to *know* God (Exod. 7:5, 17; 8:6, 18; 9:14, 29; 11:7; 14:4, 18). This reminds us that in addition to the national or particularistic purpose of the Exodus in God's scheme, it also has a conscious universalistic purpose, and that both of these elements were equally emphasised in Israel's understanding of its origins.

We are dealing with the politics of a new power structure. In such circumstances the approach to the Israelites becomes clearer. The overt reason for concern about them, their increasing numerical strength and the risk that they will become a fifth column, may well reflect some political reality, but is nevertheless very close in tone to Haman's incitement of Ahasuerus (Esther 3:8–9) and similar ploys throughout history by regimes seeking a scapegoat to help secure their own position of power. Even the phraseology 'come let us deal wisely with them' (Exod. 1:10) and the subsequent plot suggest a secret and unprovoked assault upon a people not otherwise considered as a threat by the general populace.

This is the reading of the subsequent events by Nachmanides (Rabbi Moshe ben Nachman, 'RaMBaN' 1194–1270) (Commentary to Exodus *ad loc*):

> Pharaoh and his counsellors did not want to slay them by the sword for it would have been a great treachery to smite for no reason a people admitted to the land by command of a previous king. Furthermore, the people of the land would not allow the king to do a violent act like that, for he was accustomed to consult with them, and all the more so since the children of Israel were a numerous and mighty people and would fight a great war against them. But he said that he would employ wisdom so that Israel would not feel that he was acting with enmity against them.
>
> It is for that reason that he imposed a levy on them, it being a custom for resident aliens to pay a levy to the king, as happened in the reign of King Solomon. Then afterwards he instructed the midwives in secret to kill the male children on the birthstool, so that even the mothers themselves would not know it. Then after that he instructed his people: 'Every male child that is born you shall cast into the Nile', (Exod. 1:22) you yourselves. In essence he did not want to command his exeuctioners to kill them with the sword of the king or to throw them into the Nile, but rather he told the people, whoever should find a Jewish child he should throw it into the Nile. And if the father of the child should complain to the king or the head of the city he would respond by asking him to provide witnesses so that he could punish the crime. Now when the king's strap was removed (i.e. the usual restrictions on injustice were set aside in the case of the Israelites), the Egyptians were free to search out houses and to enter them by night and with complete unconcern (lit. making themselves strangers), take the children out from there.

There are chilling similarities between Nachmanides' reading and the stages whereby the Nazis first disenfranchised, then gradually robbed their Jewish citizens of their status as human beings, thus freeing people from any sense of remorse about mistreatng them. Other commentators increase the stages of this subjugation by seeing in 1:11–14 a gradual worsening of the work to which they were subjected with its subsequent degradation.

A further stage of subjugation is created in which Egyptian taskmasters employ Israelite 'foremen' to rule over their fellow Israelite slaves (Exod. 5:14). This is a familiar policy of divide and conquer, of alienating one particular class from the rest of the populace by giving them a higher status and making them dependent on the ruling power both to maintain their position and protect them from the anger of their own people. An additional effect is to provide a buffer group between the subjugated and those who wield the real power. The biblical account provides in brief but clear images a sharp picture of a hierarchical, repressive regime. Whether it accords with a 'real', recoverable Egyptian society may be difficult to assess, but from the point of view of the narrative that was to become scripture, this is part of the 'truth' of the Egyptian bondage.

The Pharaoh who deals with the returning Moses is no less a subtle political animal than his predecessor. When confronted by Moses' initial demand, in addition to dismissing this unknown 'god', he proceeds to undermine this potentially dangerous new leadership by increasing substantially the burden of the work and hinting that it is all because of the dangerous initiative of Moses. He does this in part by twice quoting Moses' own words, the second time rubbing it in (compare 5:17 and 5:8 with 5:3). This further policy of divide and conquer seems to prove successful as indicated by the bitter greeting Moses receives from the foremen (5:21).

These precise distinctions between the various participants in the story are very important and should not be glossed over. Because with God's response through the plagues a process is initiated in which Pharaoh in turn is gradually separated from different sections of his own society and ultimately isolated. The same ploy of divide and conquer comes back against him. If that represents the inner political strategy of God against Pharaoh, its broader lesson for the Israelites is to recognise differentiated groups among the Egyptians. It is to these fine distinctions that they are to respond and there can be no single wicked 'Egypt' as the focus of hatred and prejudice.

2. THE PLAGUES

The narrative about the plagues is very carefully constructed around a recurrent threefold pattern. In each cycle, the first plague is announced by a warning to Pharaoh in the morning (blood, swarms, hail); the second in each cycle is also preceded by a warning (frogs, pestilence, locusts); the third in each cycle has no warning before it (gnats, boils, darkness). The three plagues in each cycle become progressively more unpleasant and the three cycles themselves become progressively more sinister, the first group making life unpleasant and uncomfortable, the second group causing sickness and damage, the third group causing danger to life, and death.

Within that pattern various other sequences work themselves out. One major topic is the magicians of Pharaoh. In the contest as it is set up,

Moses stands in opposition to Pharaoh (a 'god' against another 'god') while Aaron, as his 'prophet' (7:1) and agent in ushering in some of the plagues, plays a role equivalent to the magicians.

These various magical acts may appear as no more than conjuring tricks, but they represent a challenge that goes to the heart of Egyptian religion and culture. They are an assault on the sources of power of that vast society with its slave economy, with its huge building projects, its technological expertise, its enormous bureaucracy, its rich cultural and artistic heritage. More precisely, the 'magicians' are the privileged 'technocrats' of that world because of their special skills. As Sarna (1987, 58–59) explains:

> Egypt, especially, was the classic land of magic, which played a central role in its religious life. . . . Human destiny was thought to be controlled by two distinct forces, the gods and the powers beyond the gods. Neither of these was necessarily benevolent. In fact, antagonism and malevolence were considered to be characteristic of the divine relationship with man. Inevitably, religion became increasingly concerned with the elaboration of ritual designed to propitiate or neutralise the numerous unpredictable powers that be. . . . The magician was an important, indeed indispensable, religious functionary. He possessed the expertise necessary for the manipulation of the mysterious powers. . . .
>
> In the light of all this, the performance of signs and wonders in Egypt on the part of Moses, and the high concentration of this motif in the story of the Exodus, admirably suit the social and religious milieu. Yet appearances are deceptive. While the actions of Moses appear to belong to the same category as those of the Egyptian practitioners, in actual fact the comparison is superficial.

As the Exodus narrative develops the power of the magicians is diminished and shown to be absurd against the real power of Israel's God. The stages are clear: they can reproduce the snakes (Exod. 7:10–12); the Nile water turning to blood is also within their competence (7:22), but that ability to reproduce what is essentially a plague is already absurd. Like the sorcerer's apprentice, the one thing they cannot do is reverse the disasters. They can similarly reproduce the frogs (8:7) but again merely adding to the disaster.

Their first real admission of defeat comes with the third plague, gnats, when they describe the event with which they cannot compete as *etzba elohim*, the 'finger of God' (8:19). But it is not clear what is the precise nuance of this phrase. Is it an acknowledgement of a divine intercession or is the term *elohim* (god) being used here in the more general sense of the phrase *yirat elohim*, 'the fear of God', as in Gen. 20:11 where it means in very broad terms moral or ethical values? (The same sense may also apply to the 'fear of God' of the midwives—Exod. 1:17.) Thus the 'finger of God' could have more or less the same sense as an 'act of god' in an insurance policy, a natural disaster beyond human control, but not yet evidence of a direct, causal intervention by God, and certainly not Israel's YHWH. Their statement would thus be a face-saving gesture before Pharaoh.

But they are not allowed to get away with this evasion. The plague of boils will actually touch them physically to the extent that they can no longer even enter the lists with Moses (9:11).

A new element enters with the fourth plague, variously translated as 'swarms of flies' or of 'wild beasts'. In this case the land of Goshen where the Israelites live is separated off and unaffected (8:23, 25). This separation will be repeated in the cattle plague of 9:4, the hail (9:26) and the darkness (10.:21). This degree of discrimination moves the events beyond a natural catalysm into a precise divine intervention, something the magicians have tried to deny.

From now on, as well, separate Egyptian groups will become more differentiated. Some of the 'servants' of Pharaoh accept Moses' word and take their cattle in to protect them from the hail (10:20). Before the plague of locusts they will start to argue with Pharaoh to let the Israelites go. As Pharaoh becomes more isolated his bargaining options diminish and his obsession seems to grow.

From this point Egypt becomes less and less a real place or nation and only the power hungry obsessiveness of its leader remains. It is one of the achievements of the narrative that the more God's power becomes manifest, the greater our sympathy grows for the Egyptian people themselves, trapped within a system that gives such absolute power to their leader.

The final plague steps out of the system of threes that has preceded it and by its very horror breaks also the pattern of graded severity that has appeared in each of the three cycles. The fact that the first-born alone are killed suggests that this is no arbitrary choice. On one level it may represent a measure for measure punishment for the slaying of the Israelite male children as attempted by the Pharaoh at the onset of the story. On another it gives an aetiological background to the role to be played by the first-born in Israel that are dedicated to God (13:11–16), and who will in turn be superseded by the Levites.

There is one interpretation of the event that should be noted for this study. It was given by Rabbi Aaron Samuel Tameret of Mileitchitz (d. 1931) who became a pacifist during World War One:

God Himself executed the judgment of death directly by His own power: 'For I will go through the land of Egypt in that night', I and not an intermediary. Now obviously the Holy One, blessed be He, could have given the Children of Israel the power to avenge themselves upon the Egyptians, but He did not want to sanction the use of their fists for self-defence even at that time; for, while at that moment they might merely have defended themselves against evil-doers, by such means the way of the fist spreads through the world, and in the end defenders become aggressors. Therefore the holy One, blessed be He, took great pains to remove Israel completely from any participation in the vengeance upon the evil-doers, to such an extent that they were not permitted even to see the events. For that reason midnight, the darkest hour, was designated as the time for the deeds of vengeance, and the Children of Israel were warned not to step outside their houses at that hour. . . .

The language itself is very precise: '. . . And none of you shall go out of the door of his house until the morning . . . that there not be in your midst the plague of the destroyer'. Which means: your abstention from any participation in the vengeance upon Egypt will prevent the plague of vengeance from stirring the power of the destroyer which is in you yourselves. . . .

3. ISRAELITE SOCIETY/EGYPTIAN SOCIETY

Israel's experience in Egypt functions as an 'anti-model' for the society Israel was to create. How far it is possible to distinguish political realities from the theological narrative that contains them remains an insoluble problem, but the following set of associations make a very powerful condemnation of the image of Egyptian society Israel opposed.

Gen. 47 relates the consequences of the famine which Pharaoh's dreams had predicted. Joseph, with full state support, had filled the store cities during the seven years of plenty. Now the seven years of famine had begun to bite and Joseph was approached by people seeking food. As the text narrates, in successive years they paid for it with their money (47:14) and their cattle (47:16–17), and ulitmately offered their bodies and their land (18–21, 23) to Pharaoh in return for food.

There is something very poignant in their desperation when they plead, v. 19: 'we ourselves and our land shall be slaves to Pharaoh'. The land and the people are to become the property of Pharaoh and the entire nation is reduced to a slave status. In contrast to this the Israelite alternative is to acknowledge that all human beings are indeed 'slaves', but 'slaves' not to any human power, but to God alone. Indeed at the heart of the struggle between Pharaoh and Moses are two utterly different perceptions of the term *eved* (slave/servant). In Pharaoh's Egypt, a slave is the lowest form of human existence. In Moses' terminology, to be a 'slave of YHWH' is the highest freedom (7:16 etc). It is as the 'slave of YHWH' that he is designated at his death (Deut. 34:5).

This radical transformation is spelled out in two verses in Lev. 25 which give provisions for the Jubilee year. In this year all land is to revert to its original owners from the period of the tribal allocations. That is to say, no one may possess the land but instead it must be regularly redistributed 'for the land shall not be sold forever, for the land is Mine, for you are strangers and settlers with Me' (v. 23). As dramatic is the command that all Israelite slaves be released in the Jubilee year, whatever the reason for which they have become slaves. No Israelite may 'own' another Israelite, for 'they are My slaves whom I brought out from the land of Egypt; they shall not be sold as bondmen' (25:42). There seems to be here a direct substitute of the Egyptian model, God replaces Pharaoh as the sole owner of all land and of all human beings. The 'one' God is the only power that can safeguard the absolute equality of all Israelites, and ultimately, given the thrust of the Genesis narratives, of all humanity.

With regard to the treatment of slaves, the model of Egyptian cruelty is consciously opposed. In Exod. 1:13, 14, the Egyptians 'made them serve (*b'farekh*), with rigour'. The same word recurs in the Jubilee legislation as a direct prohibition (Lev. 25:43, 46, 53). 'You shall not rule over him *b'farekh* with rigour'. Significantly, also, the first legislation recorded after the giving of the Ten Commandments, which is presumably meant to be the first set of laws of the covenant itself, is the law limiting the period of slavery to six years. Once again the social lessons to be drawn from the Egyptian experience have been separated from any emotional feelings against Egypt and instead have entered into Israel's legislative structure.

4. REMEMBER YOU WERE SLAVES . . .

The astonishing thing about the record of the Egyptian experience in Exodus, and ultimately elsewhere in the Hebrew Bible, is the sympathy that is retained for the Egyptians despite the suffering and horror contained within the events. From the experience of slavery there are lessons to be drawn—about giving rest to your own servants (the Ten Commandments) and about the proper treatment of your own hebrew slaves and of the 'stranger' within your territory. Your Israelite society is meant to express a total contrast with that of Egypt. But nevertheless the Israelites should not despise an Egyptian, because you were settlers with them once, moreover, unlike the case of the Moabites and Ammonites, an Egyptian may enter the house of Israel after the third generation (Deut. 23:8–9).

Perhaps the roots of this familiarity are already expressed within the Exodus narrative itself. The rescuer of Moses, the future saviour and creator of the nation, is Pharaoh's daughter. The 'Hebrew midwives' might be either Israelites or Egyptian 'midwives of the Hebrews'.

Similarly towards the end of the story comes the episode of leave-taking and the presents pressed on the Israelites by their Egyptian neighbours. There are questions about what precisely happened—did Israel 'borrow' under false pretenses or 'ask' what everyone knew would not be returned? That God gave the Israelites favour in the eyes of the Egyptians is beyond dispute (11:3; 12:36). More problematic is the phrase that they 'bespoiled' the Egyptians (12:36), variously understood as they 'stripped' them, or 'emptied them out'. This can be seen as either evidence of a triumphal departure or a final revenge (to be later paid for in the ornaments that went to build the Golden Calf!) or as the acquiring of wages for several centuries' unpaid labour, on the lines of Israel's own laws about what was to be paid to a slave on his release (Deut. 15:13–15):

When you set him free do not let him go empty-handed. Load him up with what you take from the flock, threshing floor and vat with which the Lord your God has blessed you. Remember that you were a slave in the land of Egypt and the Lord your God redeemed you; therefore I command you this thing today.

But there is another way entirely to read the verb here translated as 'spoil'. In its commoner form it is used of 'snatching' someone out of danger, of 'rescuing'. The same verbal form occurs in Ezek. 14:14: 'Even if these three men, Noah, Daniel and Job, were in (the land) they, with all their righteousness, would only be able to *rescue* themselves. . . .' By this reading, the Israelites 'saved' the Egyptians by claiming their wages or by accepting presents from them so that they parted in the final moment as friends.

Whether this final interpretation is true to this immediate text is hard to say. Nevertheless what does emerge from this study is the surprising sympathy felt for the Egyptians within this narrative, the Hebrew Bible as a whole and in later Jewish tradition. From the various elements we have uncovered it seems clear that the Exodus 'saved' Israelites and Egyptians alike. The achievement of the narrator has been to transform what might have been a mere triumphalistic account of an enemy vanquished and freedom gained into a symbolic struggle between two concepts of the human-divine relationship and two understandings of human society that derive from them. It is that universal significance that makes the Exodus narrative a touchstone and a penetrating challenge for invidividuals and societies alike until today.

Bibliographical Note

N. M. Sarna *Exploring Exodus: The Heritage of Biblical Israel* (New York 1987).

Hans-Winfried Jüngling

The Religious Ambiguity of the Davidic-Solomonic State

THE TENTH century BC is of crucial importance for the history of Israel. This judgment is not only that of the modern historian, but is suggested by biblical tradition itself. It presents this epoch in unusual breadth. The material fills two and a half books in the existing Old Testament: 1 and 2 Sam. and 1 Kings 1–14. The predominantly narrative material contained in these books is not homogeneous, and it is not just that it comprises a wide variety of literary forms which still reveal their origins in the oral tradition. It is also important in our context to perceive that the material contains texts viewing the events of that century from contrasting points of view and therefore arriving at completely different judgments on that period. Uncritical evaluation of the source material for reconstructing historical events is therefore from the outset precluded by the nature of that material.

In acknowledging also the challenge that the nature of the biblical texts presents to historical criticism, the following must be considered. If the historian reflects pure fact, the subject of the varied and contradictory reports and narratives, then the accumulation of narrative material seems not inappropriate, even if the impression does come to mind that in comparison, the narrative exposition of the Old Testament credo—the set phrase for the *bringing out*, 'I am the Lord your God, who brought you out of the land of Egypt, out of the house of bondage' (Exod. 20:2)—appears positively modest (Exod. 1–15). But after all, with the story realised in 1 Sam. to 1 Kings 14, we are dealing with the portrayal of the introduction, consolidation and first crises of the kingdom in Israel. The Benjaminite

Saul is the first king. His kingdom, although already basically with dynastic aspirations, is still without a firm foundation. It is David, the Judaean, who succeeds in consolidating the kingdom. Under him it gains attributes appropriate to this ancient middle eastern institution: 'Israel' (i.e. the southern kingdom of Judah, the northern kingdom of Israel and Jerusalem as unified entities of importance) is now a major society inhabiting a country with well-defined and protected frontiers. It has in the king a central authority able to assert its will to shape society both internally and externally by means of a hierarchically structured bureaucracy and military. These attributes justify speaking of the organisation established by David as of a 'state'. Old Testament academic literature in fact shows that it considers the 'introduction of the kingdom' to be synonymous with the 'introduction of the State'.

As the institution of the kingdom, introduced by Saul and secured by David—this would probably emerge from the sources without any doubts attached—really does represent something new in Israel, it may be assumed at the outset that there were supporters and critics of this new entity—in the same way as voices were probably raised advocating a conciliatory position. Biblical tradition in fact offers examples of these three reactions to the new situation. There is then only the difficult question as to which voice is the contemporary one. Too hasty an answer would probably be one which divides the source material as follows: (a) those texts which take a positive view of the kingdom and see in its introduction proof of Yahweh's historical might, are the contemporary ones and, because they are close in time to the events, they are more or less reliable sources; and (b) those texts which take a negative view of the kingdom, which denounce the human kingdom as conflicting with Yahweh's kingdom over Israel, are later thoughts, with depressing experiences of this institution in mind, thoughts whose value as a historical source must be judged at the outset with extreme caution. Recent research on the books of Samuel cast grave doubts on this simple division. To take one example, the best known: the events whereby Saul became king are portrayed and are judged in their portrayal quite differently. The two stories, 1 Sam. 9:1–10:16 and 1 Sam. 11 are favourable to the king and have an archaic character; they therefore are to be considered as old texts. 1 Sam. 8 and 1 Sam. 12 contain harsh criticism of the institution of 'the kingdom' and reveal characteristic features of deuteronomic revision; for that reason alone they are to be classified as a later product. The facts in 1 Sam. 8–12 are very much more complicated. So, in the deuteronomically revised chapter, 1 Sam. 8, in verses 11–17, an old document seems to exist which characterises the king as purely and simply *taking*. This 'king's right' has the same characteristic style as

Jotham's parable (Judg. 9:7–15) which is fundamentally ill-disposed towards the kingdom. On the other hand it has become ever clearer in recent research history that those parts in 1 and 2 Sam. which one is inclined to consider as old and even contemporary texts in no way give an objective picture of the events leading to the kingdom, rather they are to be understood to a large extent as propaganda in favour of the kingdom. Texts like this indicate by their very existence that, among people confronted with the new institution, there were groups who had to be won over by these texts to what was new. A tendentious document of this kind would probably be the collection of stories called, in research, 'the story of the rise of David' (1 Sam. 16–2 Sam. 5). Among the presumably old texts which are not only incorporated in more recent surroundings, some can however also be found with a clear tendency to be critical of the 'king. The Yahwist historical work is an example of that.

From the wealth of possible material, I should like to consider in more detail two attitudes to the state established by David. In the first, let us examine the assessment of the kingdom as it is reflected in the narrative of the David and Bathsheba scandal (2 Sam. 11–12). In the other I should like to comment on the attitude of the prophet Isaiah to the Davidic kingdom.

1. THE ASSESSMENT OF THE KINGDOM IN THE NARRATIVE 2 SAM. 11–12

These chapters tell of David's adultery with Bathsheba, wife of Uriah the Hittite, and of his manoeuvres leading to the death of Uriah (2 Sam. 11). David's crime is severely criticised by Nathan. David accepts the criticism and acknowledges his guilt. Nathan therefore grants him Yahweh's forgiveness, but foretells the death of the son born of his adultery. David undertakes fasting rites until the sick son dies. After the child's death he consoles himself and Bathsheba. She becomes pregnant again and gives birth to a son. His name is Solomon (2 Sam. 12:1–25). We do not hear of Solomon, his mother Bathsheba and Nathan again until 1 Kings 1. The narrative is fitted into the context of a campaign against the Ammonites (2 Sam. 10:1–19; 11:1 and 12:26–31; cf. also 2 Sam. 8:3–8). Yet it does not seem possible to isolate the report of the war against the Ammonites from 2 Sam. 11:2–12:25, as the siege of the city of Rabbah in the context of the Ammonite war is an important element in the narrative of David's crime (11:6–25). The complex 2 Sam. 10–12 emerges as a self-contained narrative.

This should be emphasised because for a long time the material of 2 Sam. 10–12 was regarded as a constituent part of the so-called history of the succession. To this work of literary origin, written for the benefit of

Solomon, one generally assigns, at an outside reckoning, the material in 2 Sam. 6; 7:9–20 and 1 Kings 1–2. Academic discussion in the last fifteen years has tended to concentrate on two questions: (1) How is the literary work to be exactly delimited? Here the question relates above all to the beginning and the end of the history of the succession. But the literary-critical isolation of the layers of revision is also discussed. (2) What is the attitude of this work to the kingdom? Of interest here are above all the positions adopted with regard to the second question. Answers can be reduced to three types: The history of the succession is basically anti-Davidic and anti-Solomonic. On the other hand we have the thesis that the history of the succession is pro-Davidic and pro-Solomonic, serving as propaganda for the recently established kingdom which is to be stabilised by this propaganda document. Still assuming that at least in the passages 2 Sam. 9–20 and 1 Kings 1–2, we are dealing with a relatively unified literary work, it was also argued that the work was pro-Davidic but anti-Solomonic.

In view of these divergent interpretations, the most recent discussion, especially in Anglo-Saxon countries, tries to approach the complex 2 Sam. 9–20 and 1 Kings 1–2 by giving them great consideration as independent narrative complexes, each making its own statement about the kingdom. The David-Bathsheba affair (2 Sam. 10–12), the David-Absalom narrative (2 Sam. 13–20) and the actual narrative of Solomon's accession in 1 Kings 1–2 are all viewed as closed narrative complexes of this kind.

My remarks on 2 Sam. 11–12 proceed from the following presuppositions: (1) It seems that only verses 12:7b–12 can be isolated in a literary-critical sense. (2) 2 Sam. 10–12 forms a closed narrative, self-sufficient, even if the premises established there certainly play a not inconsiderable role in 1 Kings 1–2. (3) A prophetically inspired narrative (2 Sam. 11:2–12:25), using royal archive material relating to an Ammonite war for its realisation (2 Sam. 10; 11:1; 12:26–31), does not seem to exist.

After this very generalised preliminary guide to research, let us follow the narrative through its crucial phases. Chapter eleven (v. 1) presents an exposition. It shows the situation which arose from David's victory over the Syrians allied to the Ammonites. The former no longer have any taste for an alliance with Ammon (2 Sam. 10:15–19). So, secure against further pacts between Ammon and the Syrians, David sends his commander Joab with his army against the now isolated Ammonites. He himself stays in Jerusalem.

After this presentation of the contemporary circumstances, which is at the outset clear and contributes an important narrative element—during the narrative of 2 Sam. 11–12 it does however become unclear how the events reported in the concluding part of the framework (12:26–31) are to be fitted chronologically into the story of adultery and birth—we now begin the narrative which concentrates entirely on the king's private sphere. For the rest of the story the verbs 'send' and 'take' are important. After David has seen the fair Bathsheba and made enquiries about her, 'So David sent messengers, and took her' (v. 4). Bathsheba does indeed 'come'. But the imperious gesture of 'taking' has pre-eminence. The woman 'was taken into Pharaoh's house' (Gen. 12:15) and 'Abimalech sent and took Sarah' (Gen. 20:2); in both of these records we hear of Sarah being in danger. Such an expression is a reminder that a king's right of disposal has no legal right. In 2 Sam. 11–12 the title of king is noticeably never directly used of David. We hear of the king's palace (v. 2, 8, 9), of the king's present (v. 8), the king's anger (v. 20) and of the king's servants (v. 24; cf. 17). Only Joab's words to the messenger who is to bring David the news of Uriah's death, refer to the message's addressee as 'the king' (v. 20). Whenever David is the subject of an action, and he is that throughout the narrative, we simply hear of David.

In the next phase of events, caused by the news of Bathsheba's pregnancy, David retains the initiative—in a weird manner. David 'sends' again (v. 6) to bring Uriah to Jerusalem and grant him home leave. During this leave David hopes to resolve the situation now complicated by Bathsheba's pregnancy. But Uriah refuses to co-operate with the king's plans. He does not go to his house and does not sleep with his wife. The course of this home leave is described in detail (v. 7–14), until David 'sends' again, this time more drastically (cf. v. 12 and 14). With his own death sentence in his hand, Uriah goes back to Joab. Only three verses are devoted to the implementation of the instructions in David's letter (v. 15–17). A final 'sending' follows. Joab 'sends' a messenger who is to inform David (v. 18). This part of the narrative is constructed according to an instructions-implementation pattern (v. 19–21 and v. 23–24). Even if the pattern is not quite maintained, the crucial sentence 'Your servant Uriah the Hittite is dead also', at the end of the message, is the same (v. 21, 24; cf. v. 17).

The messenger's audience with David closes with the latter's cynical remarks, that Joab shouldn't let the matter trouble him, because the sword devours now one and now another, and with orders to Joab to carry on the fight valiantly (v. 25).

The conclusion of the story of the crime once again brings Bathsheba to the fore. She hears the news and mourns. After her mourning 'David sent and brought her to his house'. The circle which began with the 'sending' and 'taking' (v. 4) is thereby closed. Bathsheba is David's wife and as such gives birth to a son.

It is true that the sentence 'she became his wife and bore him a son'

(11:27a) could be continued directly by 12:15b: 'And the Lord struck the child . . . and it became sick'. Indeed, even better would be the continuation of 11:27a by 12:24f.: 'and [she] called his name Solomon. And Yahweh loved him, and sent a message by Nathan the prophet; so he called his name Jedidiah, because of Yahweh'. It is just this last hypothetical continuation that would represent a splendid anti-Solomon birth-story. He is the son of David's adulterous relationship with Bathsheba. One cannot imagine a harsher criticism of Solomon who finally ends up on the throne. And if this birth-story belonged also to the succession-story—unthinkable in fact.

It must however be said that not even the small cut, targetted on the complex 11:27b–12:15a, can be justified in a literary-critical context. The sentence 11:27b 'But the thing that David had done displeased Yahweh' is not a sign of a later revision, as the appearance of the same wording in 11:25 proves.[1]

After David had sent in 2 Sam. 11 (v. 1, 3, 4, 14, 27) and likewise Bathsheba (v. 5) and Joab gave orders to 'send' 9v. 6, 18, 22), now Yahweh himself 'sends' (12:1).

That is the end of David's arbitrary decreeing. True, he will once again rebel and try to seize the initiative for himself; but this is the last act which convicts him.

Nathan comes to David and tells the story of the rich man and the poor man living together in a city (12:1–4). The nature of this section we shall discuss from the point of view of its form. Functionally, it can safely be described as a paradigm of justice. The story of the rich and the poor man elaborates strongly the contrast between the two. In doing so, it is noticeable how very much the story uses verbs with emotional overtones. The relationship of the poor man to the single little lamb he has bought is characterised as personal by the choice of vocabulary (he brought it up, it grew up with his children, ate of his morsel, drank from his cup). The sequence reaches an erotic note: 'and lie in his bosom'. It concludes with the words: 'It was like a daughter to him'.

The relationship of the rich man to his possessions is also brought home to the listener by an expression marking strong emotions. So, when the rich man receives a visit, 'he was unwilling to take' any of his livestock or cattle. The expression used here is completely unusual and there is no question that full emphasis is placed on the wording, stripped of its familiarity, 'he was unwilling to take'.[2] In this wording speaks the self-centredness of the rich man. If he cannot bring himself to 'take' anything from himself, then he is unscrupulous enough to be ready to 'take' from the poor man.

It is certainly a case of justice. But the case itself would probably not be so serious if it were not drawn into the realm of humanity by the story itself. What is crucial in this story is the working out of just that deeply human relationship between the poor man and is lamb and the deeply inhuman self-pity of the rich man, because of which he is incapable of giving, only able to take. The whole story which Nathan tells here is determined by the humanism of the Old Testament and the wisdom of the Middle East. The word-pair used, 'rich-poor', is typical of the terminology of the Book of Proverbs. The story brings to life the words of the proverb: 'The rich rules over the poor and the borrower is the slave of the lender' (Prov. 22:7). What the proverb prosaically identifies as the rich being master over the poor, Nathan's story works out in its emotional and human dimensions.

The word 'take' determines Nathan's story. The rich man is a 'taker'. David himself 'sent' and 'took' Bathsheba (11:4). If, in the course of the narrative of his crime, David was only indirectly represented as king, but nevertheless presented as the 'taker', then, in the section 1 Sam. 8:11–17, 'taking' is shown as a typical attribute of the king. There, the 'taking' of the king leads inevitably to the enslavement of those from whom he takes. On the other hand, Samuel, who played a part in Saul's progress to the kingship, did not *take* (1 Sam. 12:3–5).

The accumulated inhumanity in Nathan's story rouses David's anger. David's answer is not completely unequivocal. Does it mean that the inhumane rich man deserves the death penalty (that is how the expression 'deserves to die' is usually understood)?[3] Is David speaking of the rich man as of a scoundrel and criminal? Judgment on the sevenfold (as the Greek textual evidence has it) or fourfold restoration (as in the Hebrew text, probably adapted there to the definition of legal consequences in Exod. 22:1) is also ambiguous. What is crucial is that David considers the rich man, presented to him in Nathan's story, as a scoundrel (or doomed to die) and liable for full restitution 'because he had no pity'. The same word occurs in the story where it was put in a similarly complicated manner, namely that the rich man 'had pity'—only with himself, not with the poor man.[4] The dense weave of the narrative can hardly be teased out analytically without losing the conciseness of the account.

After David's response has reached the crucial word in Nathan's story, comes David's exposure: 'You are the man' (12:7).

After such an exposure an explanation on the part of Nathan would not appear superfluous. Particularly as in the piece, structured by means of the passenger formula (v. 7b and v. 11), we twice find the verb 'take' (v. 9, 10), of such importance for the story so far. In the prophetic words there could indeed still be some information like that by way of explanation and justification by Nathan. But it seems impossible to untangle it in a literary-critical manner from the prophetic words which open up the prospect for what, from 2 Sam. 13 onwards, we will be told about David's family relationships which will endanger the stability of the kingdom. For the rest, we can rely on such a concise narrative to make do without any express justification of Nathan's words of exposure.

Just as concise as Nathan's exposure of David, which is at the same time an accusation, is David's answer: 'I have sinned against the Lord' (v. 13a).

Nathan promises David forgiveness for his sin (or, the sin is transferred to another). David himself will not die, but the child will (v. 14).

At this point let us break off our consideration of the narrative. What can be deduced from it in respect of its attitude to the king and the kingdom? The answer depends on how each exegete places the narrative in a literary-historical context. We have touched on that already. A different answer will emerge according to whether the interpreter considers it to be a prophetic narrative, focusing on David less as a person and more as a type, or a narrative which is close chronologically to the events and whose material must first be accepted as an occurrence.

With regard to the interpretation of the narrative as a composition expressing protest against the kingdom of Israel and Judah, dating possibly from the middle period of the Kings the questionable literary-critical treatment leading to this view must be advanced as a counter-authority.

It probably seems more sensible to take the narrative in 2 Sam. 11–12 as what it claims to be: a portrayal of events in the life of David. The question is, however, which? Only David's crime and the illegitimate birth of Solomon (if we cut the passage 2 Sam. 11:27b–12:24a)? It is not open to any doubt that the story of a crime like this seems particularly obvious to modern critical man because of his belief that the institution and the apparatus are capable of anything. Such a reconstruction arouses mistrust because it corresponds particularly to modern expectations of power.

The narrative must be interpreted in the same way as it can be investigated in its original state on the basis of more or less certain criteria. It thereby emerges with great probability that the narrative contains both David's enormous inhumanity which gives free rein to his arbitrary behaviour (2. Sam. 11) *and* how a man of power finds his own way back to a humanity based on the confession of his sin before Yahweh (2 Sam. 12).

The narrative of 2 Sam. 11–12 is again probably more clearly defined when seen in relation to the tendentious story in Judg. 19:1–30a and its laconic commentary in Judg. 21:25: 'In those days there was no king in Israel; every man did what was right in his own eyes.' It is with this assumption (cf.

Judg. 19:1) that we read the narrative of the hideous crime beginning with the violation of hospitality and ending with mass rape and the death of the raped woman. The crime committed against the Levite's wife and the Levite in Gibeah, Saul's homeland—a crime unparalleled in history—would not have happened if the Levite had spent the night in Jebus, i.e. in Jerusalem, where there would have been hospitality and the rule of law because of the king. The tendentious story in Judg. 19 makes it most abundantly clear that since there is a kingdom in Jerusalem, there is law and order. The kingdom is an authority defending people against arbitrary behaviour and chaos. It is directed against groups clearly hostile to the kingdom, possibly of a basically antithetical outlook, not only towards the Jerusalemite kingdom.

What we hear of David in 2 Sam. 11:2–27a, sounds almost like a narrative originating in such circles. The king is not a guarantor of justice and order, but is instead, in the worst possible way, the source of chaos. His actions have nothing in common with what royal ideologues propagate as the task of the occupant of the throne—action for justice and righteousness (cf. Ps. 72)—instead he behaves like a man who takes, in arbitrary fashion, without justice and righteousness, without the slightest trace of solidarity with his fellow human beings.

But the presentation of David as an exponent of an institution that virtually only takes, is only one side. However much in the narrative of 2 Sam. 11 David is depicted as a despot walking over corpses, how much then does the second part of the narrative show that a man, a master of institutionally secured power structures, also does not turn a deaf ear to words exposing and criticising him and has at his disposal a necessary measure of willingness to be taught.

This may appear strange to the modern observer who takes it as given that it is just those exponents of power who are immoveable and unteachable, unable to accept criticism. If the narrative in 2 Sam. 11–12 shows David as ready to break the law *and* capable of being criticised, then this narrative surely touches on something really very human and beyond that, possibly portrays the man David who consolidated the institution of the kingdom in Israel.

It was said above that David, by organising a standing army and a bureaucracy, introduced State structures which made it possible for him as central authority to enforce the will which shaped Israel's society. It is probable that he was able to fall back on many of the organisational circumstances of Jebusite Jerusalem. The organisation of the kingdom also came about through the adoption of the king's ideology as it is more or less reflected in Ps. 2 or 2 Sam. 7:14. An indispensible part of the king's ideology is his concern that the weaker should not succumb to the stronger (cf. Ps.

72). The origins of this kingdom may have prevented two different things: (a) The kingdom in Israel never reached a position of acting as mediator with God himself. The sacred aspect of the kingdom remained limited. (b) Connected with that is the fact that the king remained exposed to criticism, possibly from the beginning and probably right throughout its history up to its end in the exile of the last descendant of David.

2. ISAIAH'S PETITION (ISA. 7)

If the section of 2 Sam. 11–12 was difficult to categorise in literary terms and even more difficult to ascribe to definite groups—are we perhaps dealing here with 'underground literature' which at a later date was brought out by the authors of the deuteronomical historical work; or are we dealing with 'court literature'?—then the so-called petition of Isaiah (Isa. 7–8) seems to represent something which was passed on in intimate circles (cf. Isa. 8;16; cf. 30:8). But we must remember that for almost forty years Isaiah accompanied the state of Judah and its capital Jerusalem with his criticism, and that not only from an 'underground' position but in all probability in public.

One striking sentence from the petition runs, 'Yahweh will bring upon you and upon your people and upon your father's house such days as have not come since the day that Ephraim departed from Judah . . .' (Isa. 7:17).

This announcement by the prophet stands in direct relationship with that which, as a sign of God to Ahaz, the king of Judah, promises the child Immanuel, born of a young woman (7:14f.). The section Isa. 7:10–17, brief but so crucial for the New Testament (Matt. 1:23; cf. Luke 1:31) and in its consequences so important for the development of christological doctrines, has to be seen together with the preceding words of Isaiah to Ahaz (Isa. 7:1–9).

The period in which the prophet speaks is indicated by verses 7:1–2: Tiglath-Pileser, the founder of the neo-Assyrian empire, has been ruling since 745 BC in Asshur. In the years around 734 the kingdoms of Damascus and Samaria try to set up an anti-Assyrian alliance to counter his expansion. The allies try to win over the southern kingdom of Judah to their side. They are ready to force Jerusalem into the alliance, even against its will. In the face of the allies' threat to Jerusalem and Judah, the prophet calls upon the king of Judah to be still and calm (7:4) and most importantly to believe (7:9). For the anti-Assyrian alliance of Samaria and Damascus will have no success.

The prophet's petition says nothing concrete about the king's political measures. But it is clear from 2 Kings 16:7–9 that Ahaz turned to the Assyrian in order to ward off the allies' threat. The price paid was Judah being dependent on Asshur. The prophet's pleading was directed against the king's political calculations.

The text of Isa. 7 shows that the king needs a second word. Acting on behalf of his God the prophet offers the king a sign which the latter may request from the underworld or from on high. When the king rejects the offer, the prophet reacts with the announcement of the sign of Immanuel. It means at one and the same time both the failure of the allied powers and their planning against Jerusalem *and* the beginning of a situation for the king, his house and his people which is as catastrophic as the division of the kingdoms of Israel and Judah, united under David and Solomon. Although there is great controversy in research surrounding discussion of the text, it probably does reveal the following to be the prophet's opinion: (a) The attempts of the allies Damascus and Samaria will come to nothing. They will fall victim to neo-Assyrian expansionism. (b) But the failure of the anti-Assyrian alliance in no way means a simultaneous promise of security for Judah-Jerusalem and its king. On the contrary: Judah-Jerusalem and the king and his house will experience a catastrophe similar in scale only to the division of the kingdom after the death of Solomon. (c) The failure of the plans of the anti-Assyrian alliance seems to be brought about by the fact that, according to Isaiah's belief, Yahweh vouches for the city he has chosen as his dwelling-place. (d) The text of the petition reveals a split between Yahweh and the king on the one hand and between king and prophet on the other. (e) The sentence 7:17 documents the fact that the split in the kingdom under Jeroboam I at the end of the tenth century, that is dating back from the time of the prophet's address to Ahaz, about two hundred years in the past, was also, in the prophet's opinion, a misfortune of great proportions. That means conversely that Isaiah views the time of the united kingdom of Judah and Israel under David and Solomon as a time of Yahweh's blessing and care.

After about two hundred years of the Judaic kingdom's history we therefore find in Isaiah a differentiated attitude to this institution and so to the Judaic state. In the one hand, Isa. 7:1–17 is evidence of the prophet's criticism voiced against the foreign policy of King Ahaz. On the other hand he is not basically in critical opposition to the kingdom in Jerusalem.

Isaiah's thinking is substantially guided by Jerusalemic theologumena. So much so that, for example, a genuinely Israelite concept like that of the Exodus from Egypt plays no part in it. Among the theological themes of Jerusalem we find: Yahweh as king (Isa. 6:5); Yahweh's holiness (Isa. 6:3), Yahweh's dwelling on Mount Zion (Isa. 8:18; cf. 28:16), Jerusalem/Zion as the home of righteousness and justice (1:21; 28:17).

Time and again justice and righteousness are set against the State and its representatives as a measure of judgment (cf. Isa. 5:7; 28:17). Whereas Isaiah's early prophecy has as its theme precisely the violation of justice and corruption of righteousness amongst the influential classes of society in Jerusalem Isa. 3:13–15; 5:1–7; 5:22; 10:1–3), for the future he expects a king whose throne is founded on justice and righteousness (Isa. 9:6–7). The question whether it will then be someone directly of David's line who will accede to David's throne must probably be answered in the negative; because Isaiah seems to have in view at the same time both continuity and discontinuity, when he speaks of a shoot from the stump of *Jesse* on whom Yahweh's spirit will rest and whose girdle will be righteousness and faithfulness (Isa. 11:1f., 5). It is therefore not David's direct descendent who will have the gift of the spirit. God will set a new beginning. Here perhaps Isaiah also has in mind that the new beginning will reach back to Jerusalem and Judah in a condition pre-dating even the introduction of the kingdom: to the time of the Judges (cf. Isa. 1:26). It is true that the discussion of 'judges' and 'counsellors' in the context of Isa. 1:21–26 is not clear. But there could still also be in this piece a return to fundamentals, a position adopted by the prophet vis-à-vis the present institutions of the State, in the sense namely that the condition of the State/king, as found by Isaiah, is presented as one that should be swept away by Yahweh's purifying judgment. That the prophet's view does in fact reach away back into the past, beyond the beginnings of the kingdom in Jerusalem, also seems to suggest the words about the day of Midian as a day of great rejoicing (Isa. 9:3–4; cf. Judg. 7).

From these fairly superficial remarks on the prophet Isaiah the following probably becomes clear: the prophet, his thoughts guided by Jerusalem traditions, sees in the time of the United Kingdoms i.e. the Davidic-Solomonic time, an ideal time. Then, Jerusalem was a city where justice and righteousness had right of residence and even in the night, the time of chaos, they were not endangered. Then, the demands of the king's ideology, in which the king enforces justice and righteousness on behalf of the poor, were met. The historical (cf. Isa. 9:8–21) and the actual experiences with the institution of the Judaic state seem crucially to have prevented the prophet from making a total identification. Unafraid, he goes towards the king and refers him to Yahweh.

Together with many others texts of pre-exilic prophets, the prophecy contained in Isa. 1–31 adopts a position half-way between negation and affirmation of the kingdom and therefore of the State. The view into the future of a king, a descendant of Jesse, on whom Yahweh's spirit will really rest and the view backwards into the past of Jerusalem as home of justice and righteousness, form the yardsticks for his criticism of the state with which Isaiah actually has to deal.

Isaiah himself became a witness of the fall of the northern kingdom. How did he react? Passages like Isa. 17:1–6 and Isa. 28:1–4 are thought to give some idea of the prophet's anguish at the aberrations of the northern state's politics.

The Judaic state was caught up in the whirlpool of political events at the end of the seventh and the beginning of the sixth century BC. Josiah's reform work remained unfinished. In the year 587 BC Judah's sovereignty is at an end, Jerusalem and the Temple are destroyed. Reflections on this catastrophe soon begin. The exilic literature is enormous—and its extent is increasing, the more that exegetes transfer literature which in earlier periods of research had been allocated according to literary-historical criteria to a pre-exilic period. Taking two texts from the Book of Ezekiel, let us see how, at this time of extreme crisis—we are talking of the late exilic and post-exilic period—a renewal was being pondered. We can see again the same approaches to the question of the State which were expressed when it began. The text Ezek. 37:15–28 presents the prophetic symbolic action of joining together two sticks representing the kingdoms of Judah and Israel so that they become one in the prophet's hand (v. 16–17). The explanation speaks of the gathering of the people of Israel from the nations, of the union of the divided kingdoms and of the one king who will rule over them (v. 21f.). This revelation of the future speaks again of Yahweh's servant David who will be king, a shepherd for them all. In this society all will observe and follow Yahweh's ordinances and statutes (v. 24). Success will come to those who live in the land which Yahweh gave to Jacob his servant and in which their fathers lived. And once again David is mentioned, now however not with the royal title but with the title 'nasi': a title probably pre-dating the State, it is difficult to construe, it already occurs in the Book of the Covenant (cf. Exod. 22:28) and is usually rendered as 'prince' (Ezek. 37:25). Does this thereby indicate a re – interpretation of the king's title and at the same time of the social system he stands for?

The second text to which I would like to draw attention is Ezek. 34. This presents the great indictment of the shepherds. Since earliest times in Mesopotamia 'shepherd' had been used as a substitute term for king. Instead of the shepherds 'feeding themselves' Yahweh himself will be the shepherd. The text outlines a future under God's rule needing no human shepherds (Ezek. 34:11–16; 17–22; 25–31). But as if to correct this picture, we then find in verses 23–24 the words about the one shepherd David, Yahweh's servant, finally called 'nasi' as in Ezek. 37:25.

The texts of hope from the exilic period document once again the struggle for the just ordering of a society which professes its faith in Yahweh that he himself will gather them together from all the nations.

Translated by Gordon Wood

Literature

F. Crüsemann *Der Widerstand gegen das Königtum. Die antiköniglichen Texte des Alten Testaments und der Kampf um den frühen israelitischen Staat* (Neukirchen-Vluyn 1978).
P. K. McCarter *II Samuel. A New Translation with Introduction, Notes and Commentary* (New York 1984).

Translator's Notes

1. This similarity of wording in German is not reflected in the RSV. In both 11:25 and 11:27 the German uses the expression *eine böse Sache in den Augen Joabs/Jahwes*, meaning literally 'a wicked thing in the eyes of . . .'.
2. The argument here and later hinges on the German expression *er hat Mitleid* (meaning literally 'he has pity'). The RSV has 'he was unwilling' in 12:4, whereas the German wording is the same in both 12:4 and 12:6.
3. The question arises because the German has *Sohn des Todes* (meaning literally 'son of death') where the RSV has 'deserves to die'.
4. See Note 2.

Bernard Renaud

Prophetic Criticism of Israel's Attitude to the Nations: A Few Landmarks

THE PROPHETIC books show Israel as having a double attitude to the nations. There is collaboration which takes the form of trade and political alliances on the one hand and, on the other, arising from her experience of subjugation and conquest, out-and-out rejection. The prophets vigorously denounce the former of these attitudes but are less virulent about the latter. Their oracles against the nations support the popular feeling of xenophobia. One risk of such proclamations is the reduction of YHWH to the rank of national god, who blindly adopts his people's cause.

In fact, prophetic thinking is subtler and more complex than it at first appears. An attentive reader of the Bible will discern a theological development. Here we look at three of its significant stages. These are the breakdown of the frontiers of the nationalist horizon; the possibility of conversion accorded to pagans; the nations' sharing in eschatological salvation.

1. ISRAEL AMID THE NATIONS (AMOS 1–2)

Israelite prophecy reaches a turning point with Amos. For the first time in history, it moves from condemnation of individuals to whole nations, including Israel herself. The effect on this is to place Israel among the nations, 'among all the families of the earth (Amos 3:2).' Thus the horizon is widened considerably. YHWH, who summons the nations to his tribunal,

35

appears here as the universal God who condemns nations in the name of a moral law, of which he claims to be the guarantor.

In fact, in Amos 1–2, the list of people judged by God is more limited than it appears. They are confined to nations constituting Judah and Israel's immediate environment. The prophet mentions neither Egypt nor Assyria, although he is aware of their existence and power (Amos 3:9). Neither does he include Calneh, whose name figures in 6:2. Moreover, if one admits, as is probable, that the oracles against Tyre, Edom and Judah derive from a later stage of the book's composition, the horizon is even more limited. What dominates the remainder is the hostility felt by these little kingdoms towards Samaria, their closest neighbour. doesn't this mean that YHWH is still figuring as a national god? Can't these condemnations be translated simply as the aggression felt by Israel towards her attackers?

However, two points should be noted to qualify this: the type of accusation contained in the oracles, and the inclusion of Israel herself in the list of peoples accused. It is very significant that the oracles against Moab (Amos 2:1–3) does not speak of attacks against Israel or Judah, but crimes committed against another pagan nation, Edom. Of course this does not mean that the other accusations are concerned only with wrongs done to foreign countries, but N. Gottwald rightly remarks that the oracle against Moab is situated at a strategic point, just before the oracle against Israel: YHWH behaves as an impartial and universal judge, who makes no distinctions. He who judges Moab for its crimes against Edom will not hesitate to condemn Israel for her own crimes.[1] In Amos 3:9–11, the prophet invites the Philistine city of Ashdod (or Assyria in the Greek translation) to look at the disorder and injustice reigning in Samaria. Doubtless this is a rhetorical device. Nevertheless it is clear that the prophet feels that the nations are no longer complete strangers to one another. The evil committed by their neighbours concerns them and YHWH may call them to witness in his trial of his people.

So, what are the minimal values apparently imposed on all the peoples of the earth? S. Amsler[2] holds that the prophet is addressing not the foreign countries but Israel. For him, the law revealed to Israel and according to which it will be judged, has a universal scope. It is not Israel that is put on the same level as the nations, but the nations which are judged by Israel's standard. Thus, Israel 'is not judged in accordance with a universal law. On the contrary, it is the justice revealed to Israel which manifests YHWH's demands on the whole of humanity.' In these oracles against the nations, the crimes involve countries as a whole, and war crimes. Then reproaches against Israel refer to the behaviour of individuals in the political, economic and social spheres (Amos 2:6–8, 12). One can think of a sort of international law, customs tacitly recognised by countries as a whole, notably in the case of conflict, a sort of good conduct code. Certain Near Eastern documents treaties or conventions seem to have conserved traces of it.[3]

At any rate, it seems clear that for Amos, YHWH's authority extends to cover international morality. He punishes sins committed, because he is interested in the fate of both individuals and nations. His solicitude goes beyond care of his chosen people. If we seek a theological foundation for this divine behaviour, we are led inevitably to the moral character of the God of Israel. Seeking YHWH is to hate evil and love good (Amos 5:4–6; 14–16).

The second original point in this text is that Israel is included in the list of peoples condemned. This raises a difficult question, because it seems to weaken the privileged status of the chosen people: 'You only have I known of all the families of the earth.' (Amos 3:2). This tension underlies the whole book of Amos and we should not lose sight of either of the two sides. How can it be resolved? In good theology, we can only speak of being chosen, in the strict sense, if a people is aware that it has a special place among other nations. This condition is fulfilled in Amos 3:2 and, it seems, for the first time in the religious history of Israel. This is due to the breakdown of traditional boundaries and the widening of the political and religious horizon shown in Amos 1–2. This theology of being chosen is the counterpart to the effort made to remove from YHWH any characteristics that are too nationalistic, and show him as the Judge of the nations. This would inevitably lead Israel to ask what, henceforce, her unique relationship with YHWH might mean, a relationship confirmed by all her traditional since the exodus from Egypt. The prophet answers: God is certainly interested in all peoples and is not afraid to intervene in their history, as is shown in Amos 9:7, but he is particularly concerned with his people, whom he has 'known' (translate 'chosen') from among 'all the families of the earth' (Amos. 3:2).

But in accordance with his representation of a 'moral' God, the prophet insists that this privilege involves obligations, serious obligations. God's declaration in Amos 3:2 sounds like a threat: 'You only have I known of all the families of the earth; therefore I will punish you for all your iniquities.' The 'therefore' seems to derive from the literary form of a judgment oracle, ensuring the passing from the accusation to the sentence of condemnation. This is a paradox! The reminder that they are chosen functions here as an accusation: salvation history becomes a history of judgment. This threat in Amos 3:2 finds an echo in the sequence of Amos 1–2, where Israel's judgment occurs as the climax of the judgments of the nations. Knowing they are the chosen people rebounds against them as condemnation. So is

Israel's chosen status annulled? No. The prophet does not question God's choice but the theological consequences the Israelites wrongly draw from it: that is to say, the dogma of an unshakeable, almost automatic security. They can only make use of the privilege of being chosen to the extent that their behaviour makes them at one with the will of their God.

Thus Amos turns Israel's view of history upside down. When they heard the prophet's first words, his listeners could feel in total agreement with this diatribe against their traditional enemies. didn't these oracles avenge the humiliations and suffering of a threatened people? But, there is a new and almost revolutionary sting in the tail. The prophet goes through his long list of those condemned until he reaches Israel and lays her very existence on the line. Thus he removes the mask of a nationalistic god, with which popular sentiment had covered YHWH's face. This self-criticism gives the God of Israel a commanding view which enables him to judge the nations. The iron law, by which the conquerors are always right and the conquered always wrong, is invalidated. The actions of both are referred to a higher court, whose judgment is founded not on human success or vengeance, but on moral criteria incumbent on all countries.

2. GOD'S TENDERNESS TOWARDS THE NATIONS

For Israel, the proclamation of the judgment constituted the final appeal to conversion.[4] Do the Oracles against the Nations have the same finality? Israelite prophecy does not seem to have asked this question at the time, because these oracles themselves were in fact addressed to Israel. A prophet from the Persian epoch will reply in the affirmative, to the great displeasure of at least some of his compatriots, if we may take Jonah as personifying the particularist and sectarian spirit. The literary form of the work is the subject of heated debate. And accordingly, there is no agreement about the central theological line. It is also possible that the book's rich message cannot be summed up in a single dominant idea.

But whatever the line of the book, it is clear that it is to do with the question of YHWH's relation to the nations and that the author's answer is wholly original: the God of the Jews shows infinite compassion for all human beings, even the guiltiest. As a conclusion, the book ends on the proclamation by YHWH himself of the mystery of his infinite mercy (Jonah 4:10). All the pagans also share this hope, the sailors (1:6) and the Ninevites (3:9). What is more, the prophet himself (4:2) tells us that this was the reason why he fled and was unfaithful to God's command. With sly humour, the book's author places upon the prophet's lips here the ancient Sinai confession of faith (Exod. 34:6–7). Furthermore, by adding to the received formula 'and who revokes his decision (his threats)', Jonah lucidly draws the obvious conclusion. Has he not himself experienced divine forgiveness (Jonah 2)? But through a short of blinkered nationalistic narrowness, he refuses to go all the way: to God's universal forgiveness. Through the parable of the castor oil plant, in a sort of *argumentum ad hominem*, YHWH, in his infinite patience, tries to convince him. He appeals to his work in creation for is it possible that God's merciful heart can abandon a hundred and twenty thousand persons to their fate, for whom he laboured (4:10–11; cf. 1:9)? The book does not give Jonah's reply. It is up to each reader to respond and to receive the great revelation of the mystery: God loves the pagans and this love has no limits.

This brings up the problem of the validity of the prophets' words. If God's heart is so tender, do their proclamations of judgment still hold good? This question worried the Deuteronomists. It is asked precisely at the point where Jonah the prophet himself is named (2 Kings 14:25–7). The choice of Jonah here must be intentional, and related to the problem being discussed. But here the problem is concerned solely with whether God will revoke his judgment on Israel. The Deuteronomic author of the book of Jeremiah widens its scope to embrace every kingdom and every nation: 'If that nation, concerning which I have spoken, turns from its evil, I will repent of the evil that I intended to do to it.' (Jer. 18:8) Here we are dealing with a problem analogous to that in the book of Jonah. In the latter case, it is YHWH who takes the initiative and sends Nineveh a prophet, as he had sent one to his own people. Just as the choice of the prophet is not neutral, neither is that of Nineveh. Had not this city left to history the memory of one of the most tyrannical and cruel empires? And now the hated Ninevites respond to the first appeal. It is impossible not to see the intended contrast with Israel's obstinate refusal to listen to the appeals of the prophets. We know that the Deuteronomic tradition has made this hardening of hearts a major theme of its theology. Jonah's behaviour, in particular, illustrates graphically the constant temptation (we have already heard Amos's denunciation in Amos 3:2; 9:7), to view Israel's election by God in too narrow and particularist to way—for this election cannot affect YHWH's liberty in history or the mystery of his love and mercy.

This is not to say that Israel's originality vanishes or that it loses its privilege of being the chosen people. The sailor's prayer (1:14) does not seem to imply conversion to the monotheistic faith, and the behaviour of the Ninevites is apparently solely on moral—rather than religious—grounds. Nevertheless, whatever its limitation, this vision goes far beyond that of Amos. God is not content to be concerned with them just in order to punish them. His care for them leads him to want their conversion and to act accordingly.

We should try to measure the theological effort required of the Israelites at the time. They had lost their political independence and the great Persian empire was threatening to swallow them up. They legitimately sought to defend their racial and religious identity (cf. the books of Nehemiah and Esdras). It is understandable that this community in moral and religious danger should feel a desire for revenge. Nevertheless from within the community a voice is raised to remind them, on the basis of their ancient confession of faith, that the foreign nations are still objects of a divine concern which known no limits. We can only admire such breadth of outlook. Israel has overcome the temptation, which kept recurring all through her history, to fall into narrow and exclusive particularism. Here prophecy itself engages in self-criticism by presenting—with wry humour— a prophet embodying this particularist spirit, and condemning him outright.

3. THE PAGAN NATIONS CALLED TO ENTER THE COVENANT COMMUNITY

As they are called to conversion, can the pagan nations receive salvation? The book of Jonah did not clearly ask this question. Among the texts answering in the affirmative, we single out Isa. 19:16–25, because it has the widest vision. It is the work of the post-exilic writer, doubtless from the Persian epoch. It complements the authentic oracle in Isa. 19:1–5 and reflects on it.

(a) The dynamic of the text

Through its implicit allusion to the day of YHWH, the formula 'in that day' projects us into eschatological times. Oddly enough, this 'day' develops, in a series of stages increasing in intensity and university.

The Judgment of Egypt (vv. 16–17)

Apparently these verses carry on the preceding oracle without interruption. They even repeat word for word a formula from the preceding oracle, which gives its central theme: 'which YHWH has purposed against them (Egypt)' (Isa. 19:12 and 17). Thus, this later writer fully assumes the condemnation of Egypt. But at the same time, we may wonder whether he does not discreetly hint at going beyond this judgment. From Second Isaiah onwards, although this negative aspect still remains, God's plan can also end in salvation (Isa. 44:24 ff; 46:9–11; cf. Pss. 13:10ff; 73:24; 106:13). So verse 17 should be translated as 'what YHWH has decided about Egypt'.

The beginnings of conversion

The poem's unity and coherence (vv. 16–25) confirm this interpretation. Verse 18 tells us that 'there will be five cities in the land of Egypt which speak the language of Canaan'—that is, Hebrew. After the exile Hebrew was superseded by Aramaic as the language in everyday use, and Hebrew reserved for the liturgy. So this means the Egyptians will share in the Yahwist liturgy, as is also suggested by the announcement that they 'will swear an oath to (not 'by') YHWH', which is equivalent to a confession of faith (Isa. 45:23; 2 Chron. 15–1:14). The figure 'five' has intrigued commentators. It may mean a small number (Gen. 41:14; Isa. 17:6) and sometimes it is a sign of abundance (Gen. 45:22,43,34) or represents a collectivity (Gen 47:2). In this case the adherence of these cities to YHWH would be full of promise for the future.

Egypt worshipping YHWH (vv. 19–22)

This future is conjured up in verses 19–20: 'There will be an altar to YHWH in the midst of the land of Egypt'. Translate: the whole country will adopt the cult of YHWH. The altar and the pillar will be 'a witness to YHWH' and remind him that they are members of his community and have the right in some way to his saving intervention when they are in trouble. YHWH will be faithful to his promise and send them a saviour.

This is the beginning of a long history, like Israel's own, of times of fervour and mutual knowledge (v. 21), that is to say of sharing and communion, but also of infidelities. If the Lord smites (v. 22) it will be because the Egyptians have sinned, but in his mercy, God will hear their cries of distress and 'heal' them. 'They will return to YHWH and he will heed their supplications and heal them'.

Religious unity in a world at peace (v. 23)

Suddenly the horizon widens even beyond Egypt, to encompass the other great political power: Assyria. In the past these two traditional enemies tore each other apart. Now they are reconciled. A new road will symbolise this fellowship. What will be its function? Trade is one possibility. But it could also be a sacred highway because it will allow the Lord of Hosts to be served with one heart and mind (cf. Prov. 3:3).

One-world community of faith (vv. 24–25)

The lack of any mention of Israel in this vision is obviously surprising. In fact it is not left out altogether: 'The land of Judah' (v. 17) is the obligatory route between Egypt and Assyria. That is why it appears logically in v. 24 but only as a 'third'. It no longer has the pre-eminence usually given to it in eschatological oracles. These three partners form a single people, although they do not lose their identity. This people will be God's people ('my people'), who will reap a universal blessing (v. 25).

(b) A problematic alliance

Nowhere else in the Bible do we find such a sweeping universalism, free of any trace of particularism or Zionism. But there is even more, as a certain number of authors have clearly shown.[5] The prophet transfers to the nations the phenomena attaching to Israel's fundamental experience: YHWH's 'raised hand (v. 16) is associated in the Exodus with the epic of the escape from the defeat of the Egyptians (Exod. 16:16–18; 15:12; cf/Isa. 11:11, 15–16; Zech. 2:13). In a particular the number five (v. 18) refers back to Josh. 10:1–27, where Israel has to confront five Canaanite kings on her entry into the promised land (the number five keeps recurring in this chapter). Thus we should read Isa. 19:18 as a taking possession of Egypt by YHWH, a sort of spiritual conquest. The mention of the altar witness (Isa. 19:20) may be an allusion to Josh. 22:26 ff., which describes the building of an altar to YHWH by Tans-jordanian tribes. 'For, said they, 'It is a witness between us (that is with the Cis-jordanian Israelites) that YHWH is God' (Jos. 22:34). The Egyptians will have an analoguous status to these tribes. Although they are outside the Promised Land, they will be full members of the Yahwist community. The location 'near the frontier' is therefore significant. The old altar witness was set up near the Jordan (Josh. 22:10), the natural frontier between Trans- and Cis-Jordan. Likewise the pillar witness in Isa. 19:19–20.

At the same time this pillar also recalls the witness stone set up by Joshua in Sichem after the renewal of the alliance (Josh. 24:26–7). But the association of the altar and the pillar is also found in the scene in Exod. 24:3–8, the conclusion of the Sinai alliance and W. Vogels 'has shown precisely how the language of Isa. 19:20–22 is copies from that of Exod. 2:23–5; 3:7–8, 12, 16–18; 6:2–8). The resumption of the sequence: smiting, healing, conversion (v. 22) also recalls the four-fold theme of the Book of Judges: sin, punishment, repentance, deliverance (or healing, cf. Hos. 6:1f). These allusion recall the alliance's underlying problems, present throughout the whole course of its history, and suggests that the Egyptians share fully in the alliance's privileges. This is confirmed by the titles given to the nations in the final blessing: 'Egypt *my people*' (cf. Exod. 3:10; 5:1; Deut. 4:20 etc.); 'Assyria the work of my hands' (cf. Isa. 60:21; 64:7; Deut. 32:8; 4:20 etc.); 'Israel *my heritage*' (Isa. 19:25). These three qualifications, almost identical in meaning, are reserved in the Bible for the *chosen people*. Here they are boldly applied to the pagan nations, who are called to join the covenant community in eschatological times.

Such a vision of the future does not cancel Israel's election. In fact, the opposite occurs: Israel's privileges are extended to other nations. Of course this involves the rejection of the nationalist, particularist view of this election, which had been held for so long. But Israel remains 'YHWH's heritage'. It has taken them many centuries to discover this universal scope of their own vocation. Here it is just a lone voice. But if we remember that this grandiose and largely disinterested vision arose from a humiliated people, deprived of all political independence, oppressed by these countries which it proclaims will one day be YHWH's people, just as Israel is, we can only marvel at its breadth and originality. Of course there are similar dreams of universal peace in the history of human thought. But given this depth of religious experience, such a vision can only be the result of a revelation. And Israel has been chosen to be the witness throughout the world to this 'mystery'—a mystery that was once hidden but now revealed: 'The pagans are called to this same heritage' (Eph. 3:5–6).

Translated by Dinah Livingstone

Notes

1. N. K. Gottwald *All the Kingdoms of the Earth* (New York, Evanston and London 1964) p. 110.
2. S. Amsler 'Amos et les droits de l'homme' in *De la Tôrah au Messie. Mélanges H. Cazelles* (Paris 1981) pp. 184f.
3. See J. Barton *Amos's Oracles against the Nations. A Study of Amos 1:2–2:5* (SOTS monograph Series 6) (1980)p. 41.
4. On the final intention of Amos's message, cf. R. Martin-Achard *Amos, l'homme, le message, l'influence* (Geneva 1984) pp. 134–142.
5. A. Feuillet 'Un sommet religieux de l'Ancien Testament. L'oracle d'Is. 19 (v. 16–25)' *Recherches de Sciences Religieuses* 39 (1951) pp. 65–87; J. Schreiner 'Segen für die Völker in der Verheissung an die Väter' *Bibl. Zeitschrift* 6 (1962) pp. 1–31; I. Wilson 'In that Day. from Text to Sermon on Isaiah 19:23–25' *Bibl.* 57 (1976) pp. 494–514; J. F. A. Sawyer 'Blessed my people Egypt. The Context and the Meaning of a remarkable passage' *Mel. McKane. A Word in Season* ed. J. D. Martin and P. A. Davies (JSOT Supplement Series 42) (Sheffield 1986) pp. 57–71.
6. See further W. Vogels *art. cit.* pp. 505–508.

PART II

New Testament

Sean Freyne

Oppression from the Jews: Matthew's Gospel as an Early Christian Response

THE PAINFUL and intractable problems of dialogue for Jews and Christians, especially in a post-holocaust world, is not made easier for either side because of the tone of many of their foundational texts. The Jewish desire to denigrate Jesus and the first Christians, expressed in certain rabbinical sources, never matured into full-scale persecution only because from the fourth century onwards Jews for the most part inhabited a Christian world as second class citizens devoid of real political power.[1] In subsequent centuries Christians have, on occasion, been only too willing to draw inspiration from their own foundational documents in order to fuel the fires of anti-semitic hatred. Paradoxically, many of those Christian texts were themselves produced in an atmosphere of Jewish social dominance, with the consequent hatred of the oppressor that such a situation engenders.[2]

If Christians today, while remaining faithful to their own religious heritage, wish to re-frame their relationship with the Jews, there is an urgent need for them to learn the often painful lessons of history—not just the history of Auschwitz, but also that of the first centuries of the common era when many of our current attitudes were fashioned and took on the guise of unchanging and unchangeable dogma. An adequate, that is, a critical history of Jews and Christians in Antiquity still remains to be written. Thankfully there are signs that in there current post-Auschwitz climate, scholars of good will on both sides are availing of the opportunity to re-examine many of the current stereotypes of the past and recognise the

47

ideological biases that are embedded in their own most sacred texts.[3] If we really believe that the truth can set us free we must be prepared to recognise that our claims on truth have also created victims and, on occasion, turned us, the oppressed, into oppressors.

Matthew's gospel provides as good a sounding board as any for testing some of these claims. Here is one of the most 'Jewish' documents of all the early Christian writings, yet no other document of the Christian canon, with the possible exception of the Fourth Gospel, is more critical of certain aspects of Jewish life and practice. It would be convenient, but not accurate to report that this document merely reflects an 'in-house' dispute similar to that reflected in the literature emanating from other branches of sectarian Judaism of the Second Temple period. Undoubtedly, as has often been noted, there are similarities of claims and rhetoric between this gospel and some of the Essene writings in particular.[4] However, with the superior self-assurance of a scribe 'discipled in the kingdom of heaven' (13:51f.), our author takes his own stance over against his former co-religionists. The story that Jesus' body had been stolen from the tomb had, he tells us, been spread abroad among the Jews to the day of his own writing (28:15). He speaks repeatedly of 'their synagogues' (4:23; 9:35; 10:17; 12:9; 13:54; 23:34), suggesting a definite distance from that institution, which at the time of writing of the gospel was in the process of becoming the alternative holy place of the Jews in the wake of the destruction of the temple in 70 CE (see 22:7). We cannot then escape the consequences that in this gospel we are encountering early Christian self-identity expressing itself with some vehemence over against the parent religion, itself in the process of redefining its centre at a critical juncture in its history.

1. MATTHEW'S CHARACTERISATION OF THE JEWS

How does this consideration express itself textually? A first step in our critical reading of Matthew must be briefly to sketch again his profile of the Jews. Since it is a recurrent pattern of human relations, especially in adverse situations, that we caricature our opponents and their arguments as a tactic of discrediting them, we must be conscious that even a Christian evangelist is not immune from such frailty.

Matthew is not so removed from the situation as to ignore all distinctions between the various groups—Pharisees, Sadducees, Scribes, elders, chief-priests and 'the crowd'—a feature of the Fourth Gospel's treatment of the Jews as is well known. Yet by a clever process of association as the narrative progresses, he is able to bring them all under the same condemnatory accusation: they are evil—their root trait, as Kingsbury calls it.[5] This trait manifests itself in various ways: blindness to the obvious presence of God in their midst (12:27f.); an ethical vision that is narrow (12:7.11), self-centred (15:3–6), even downright hypocritical (23:13–31); a hostility towards those who do not share their point of view (10:17.23; 23:32–36); a lack of concern for the religious and social needs of those in their charge (9:36); an inability to understand their own scriptures, despite their claims to be authoritative teachers of God's will (9:13; 12:3.5.7; 21:16.42; 22:29.31).

It is indeed a formidable catalogue of charges, but without any irrefutable evidence being provided other .than a series of pictures of various groups appearing throughout the narrative, that, at best, are so selective as to be downright distorting.

The tone for the subsequent treatment is set in the opening chapters. The Jewish religious leaders, and indeed 'all Jerusalem' share Herod's foreboding about the birth of the child Jesus. This is condemnation by association with a brutal and selfish king. Next, in a totally unprepared outburst, the Pharisees and Sadducees together, without any differentiation between their attitudes, are made to bear the brunt of John the Baptist's trenchant attack. For the ideal reader this is the signal for the release of pent-up feelings of anger at the very first opportunity and it does not forebode well for what lies ahead (3:7–12). They are identified in sub-human categories as a brood of vipers—a standard vituperative ploy in all cultures, which the main character also uses later in identifying their real problem as the author sees it: 'Brood of vipers! How can you speak good when you are evil?' (12:34).

This condemnation, the apocalyptic tones of which are quite clear, brings into the open attitudes in the Jewish leaders which the author/narrator had already drawn to the attention of the ideal reader, but which had not yet lead to open confrontation. The scribes had thought in their hearts that Jesus was blaspheming (9:3), and the Pharisees had declared in an aside that his cures were achieved through the ruler of the demons (9:34). Eventually, they make the public accusation of Jesus being in league with Beelzebul, the prince of demons (12:24).

It is this that provokes the main character to declare that they are evil. This judgment is followed by a number of images which illustrate the eschatological consequences of their condition. Their evil word is a sign of the evil treasure in their hearts, a conscious contrast with the Christian scribe who can bring forth treasures new and old (13:51f.). Since it is by their words that that will be either justified or condemned, their fate is already sealed. Later, scribes and Pharisees together are designated as plantings which the heavenly Father has not planted and which will therefore be rooted out, that is, in terms of the author's imagery, committed to final destruction (cf. 13:24–30, 37–43). This judgment on their condition is because they *are scandalised* at Jesus's teaching on what is significant in determining God's will (15:13f.), and ironically, as the ideal reader perceives, they are thereby excluded from the blessing which had earlier been promised to those who were not *scandalised* at his coming (11:6).

It is in Jerusalem that the most sustained attack on the Jewish religious leaders is mounted. Matthew weaves an intricate combination of audiences to ensure that all the various groupings of Jewish religious leadership hear the parables of condemnation and the sevenfold set of woes on the scribes and Pharisees, hypocrites (21:28–22:14; 23:13–35). These final scenes of condemnation take place, fittingly from the author's point of view, in the temple, since the judgment on faithless Israel is also a judgment on its religious institutions, symbolised most poignantly in the destruction of Jerusalem, the holy city (21:43; 23:36–39).

Throughout the narrative, 'the crowd' plays an interesting middle role between Jesus and the false teachers of Israel. It is not as colourfully portrayed as in Mark, and the crowd's enthusiasm during the Galilean phase of the story is more restrained. Yet they show their admiration for Jesus' teaching after the Sermon on the Mount, contrasting it favourably with that of their own scribes (7:27). Later, they are declared 'sheep without a shepherd', but sadly in danger of becoming 'the lost sheep of the house of Israel' (9:36; 10:6; 15:24). Even in Jerusalem they continue to hail Jesus as a prophet (21:8–11.46; 22:23), just as they had done earlier in Galilee (9:8; 12:23; 15:31). Yet even then an ominous note is struck for the attentive reader. As the prophet/servant, Jesus' ministry must include the nations 'who hope in his name' (12:18–21), and the Galilean towns are condemned for their failure to understand his mighty deeds, no less than Jerusalem (11:20–24). Thus, it comes as no major surprise to the ideal reader that in the end the crowd comes under the control of the opponents (27:20), and formally, as the people of God, they call down the blood curse on themselves in what the author wishes to suggest is a derogation of the Sinai covenant (27:25; cf. Exod. 24:8). Unlike the Lukan crowd, they do not repent subsequently (Luke 23:48), but instead they become the Jews', whereas the religious association of God's people implied in the term Israel passes to those from all the nations who are prepared to accept the teaching of Jesus (28:15–20).

2. ATTEMPTING A CRITICAL APPRAISAL

Only a nodding acquaintance with Jewish life and history of the Second Temple period—its philosophies and its pieties—is required in order to recognise this account for what it is: a sustained attack on 'other' Jewish groups, especially those associated with the scribes and the synagogues, in order to lay sole claim to being the true Israel.[6] 'History' is here being used by Matthew as propaganda, even though it can be described as 'sacred history' (*Heilsgeschichte*), since it represents his interpretation, however misguided, of the plan of God for history coming to completion in his own community's life and experience.

How are we to characterise this portrayal and its underlying strategy, particularly in view of the fact that the author claims to be 'the scribe discipled in the kingdom', who can, therefore, articulate the kingdom values of peace-making and love of enemies (5:9.38–46), as treasures that reflect the new and hidden depths of God's will revealed in the career of Jesus? Could not his words against the Jewish leaders be categorised as coming (rather) from the treasure of the evil, rather than the good man (12:35), despite the claims to the contrary expressed at 13:51f.?

It would be a mistake to attempt to exonerate Matthew by simply pointing to the situation of persecution that members of the community for which he wrote had experienced and were experiencing. In view of the eschatological claims that are being made for the ethical code which is presented as revealed wisdom expressing the Father's will in a definitive manner over against the scribes and Pharisees—ironically designated 'the wise and understanding' (11:25–27)—it is scarcely adequate to claim that Matthew's characterisation of the Jews is the direct result of the community's treatment at their hands. In fairness it must be said that many of the pejoratives which are used against the Jews can also be turned against members of his own community. They too must be warned of hypocrisy and self-serving (6:1–19; 18), and eschatological judgment—'weeping and gnashing of teeth' is the repeated expression—is a danger for all, Jew and Christian alike (8:12; 22:13; 25:30). The gap between ideal and performance is a Christian failing also and despite the apocalyptic tones, Matthew is a realist on ethical issues. (See 13:24–30, 36–43, 47–50). If his evaluation of the scribes and Pharisees' performance of God's will is less than favourable, he can still recognise their significance as authentic interpreters of Moses (23:3). It is apparently on the contrast between Moses and Christ that he wishes to base his own claims to superior knowledge of God's will and therefore to the claim to a superior righteousness (5:17–20) and a perfection that goes beyond the Law (19:16–30).

Attention has already been drawn to the rhetoric that Matthew employs and to its social function. He combines features of vituperative polemics, like unfavourable comparisons (*synkrisis*), as these were taught in the handbooks of rhetoric such as the *Ad Herrenium* of Cicero, with apocalyptic imagery of downright hatred of the perceived enemy.[7] Such imagery is born of a situation which combines a sense of intense alienation and a dualistic understanding of the world.[8] From that perspective there is little room for reconciliation or possibility of 'loving the enemy' in the present. Indeed one must ask whether Matthew saw this injunction as stretching to the enemy without or merely encompassing the alienated brother or sister within.[9] Ancient rhetoric did have a powerful political function in terms of building up one's own social identity at the expense of the enemy. Even if this means that the ancients themselves did not take such rhetoric literally in a personal way, it scarcely makes it more acceptable in terms of the ideals of Christian speech as Matthew himself articulates them: 'Let your speech be yes when you mean yes and no when you mean no. Anything that is over and above this is from the evil one' (5:37).

If then we cannot whitewash Matthew's treatment of the Jews either on historical or rhetorical grounds in view of his own stated ideals, how are we to relate to his statements on Jewish/Christian relations, we who hear his vituperations with more sensitive ears, hopefully, because of the tragedy to which this text too has contributed in our own time as part of the history of its effects? At least we cannot continue to live with Matthew's vision of salvation history, as though salvation had in fact passed from Jerusalem definitively. Justin Martyr, the second century apologist of Christianity, whose argument for the truth of Christian claims over against the Jews owes so much to Matthew, can end his dialogue with Trypho, the Jew, on a much more conciliatory note than does the Evangelist:: 'Now Trypho paused somewhat, and then said: You see that it was not by design that we fell into a discussion over these matters . . . For we have found more than we expected or than it was possible for us to expect. And if we could do this more frequently we should receive more benefit, while we examine the very words of Scripture for ourselves. But since you are putting off to sea and expect to start your voyage any day, do not scruple to think of us as your friends when you take your departure'.

Thus, later Christian experience, while sharing Matthew's claims about Jesus, can still see the possibility for dialogue in the changed circumstances of the second century, just at the point when the Judaism that Matthew had railed against was beginning to find a new self-confidence in the scribal schools of Galilee. This would eventually flower into the production of the Mishnah, the foundation document of rabbinic Judaism about the year 200 CE. Such developments should encourage us also to enter into critical dialogue with this and other early Christian texts, in our very changed situation today, as Judaism and Christianity have developed their independent systems of sanctification and salvation. Indeed, on re-reading

Matthew, it seems both possible and proper to find there some expression of hope in his vision of Israel's fate. Embedded in the lament for doomed Jerusalem is the declaration: 'You shall not see me again until you say: "Blessed is He who comes in the name of the Lord" ' (23:39). A future for Jerusalem beyond the ruins of the present seems to be expressed here, saving Matthew, ultimately, from the narrowness of a purely sectarian point of view.[10]

To be sure, when we read Matthew, especially as Christian Scripture, we are in danger of hearing only one side of an argument and reading it as though it were a definitive and absolute statement. No doubt, his less than appreciative view of his opponents was countered by their view of him and his community. While an argument from silence is never wholly convincing, nevertheless a plausible case can be made that several of Matthew's most strident claims from a Jewish point of view were prompted as retorts to counter-claims of 'the synagogue across the street'. In such a climate there is little possibility of acknowledging the other side's good faith. Even worse, that is not the context in which one's own tenuous understanding of the truth can be properly assessed and critically evaluated. Had Matthew, who proudly claims a scribal role for himself, heeded the advice of another scribe, the Jerusalemite Ben Sirach, about the need for careful speech, because of the social and political dangers of an ill-chosen word (Sirach 5:11–6:17; 8:5–7; 28:14), rather than indulging himself in apocalyptic rhetoric of destroying the enemy verbally, his statement of Christian claims might have been more nuanced and less self-assured and exclusivist. Truth claims are indeed always vitally important, not least because of our deep-seated desire for freedom. Perhaps a critical reading of Matthew can teach us that the greatest need to be self-critical is precisely at the point where we wish to make the most explicit claims to truth. The truth will only set us free when at the same time we continue to ask—not with the dismissive tones of a Pilate, 'What is truth?' Only then can we prevent the truth that liberates us from becoming the ideology that enslaves others.

Notes

1. E. Bammel 'Christian Origins in Jewish Tradition', *NTS* 13 (1967) 317–335.
2. With reference to Matthew's gospel see D. Hare *The Jewish Persecution of Christians in the Gospel according to St Matthew* (Cambridge 1967).
3. See for example the highly informative collection of essays, the result of a week-long colloquium between Jewish and Christian scholars organised by Professor Jacob Neusner at Brown University, R.I., entitled '*To See Ourselves as Others See Us*'. *Christians, Jews, 'Others' in Antiquity*, Scholars Press Studies in the Humanities

(Chico, California: Scholars Press 1985). Neusner's application of critical methods to the Jewish sources opens up new possibilities for Christian scholars, long accustomed to employing similar methods in the study of the Bible.

4. J. Gnilka 'Die Kirche des Mattäus und die Gemeinde von Qumran' *BZ* 7 (1963) 43–63.

5. J. Dean Kingsbury 'The Developing Conflict between Jesus and the Jewish Leaders in Matthew's Gospel. A Literary Critical Study' *CBQ* 49 (1987) 57–73, especially 59f.

6. See S. Freyne 'Vilifying the Other and Defining the Self. Matthew's and John's Anti-Judaism in Focus' in *'To See Ourselves as Others See Us'* 117–143.

7. Freyne 'Vilifying the Other' 118f.; A. Wilder 'The Rhetoric of Apocalyptic' in *Jesus' Parables and the War on Myths* (London 1982) 153–168.

8. G. Stanton 'The Gospel of Matthew and Judaism' *BJRL* 66 (1984) 264–284, especially 278ff., draws attention to the importance of apocalyptic mentality and motifs in Matthew's anti-Jewish polemic.

9. R. Horsley 'Ethics and Exegesis. "Love your Enemies" and the Doctrine of Non-Violence', *JAAR* 54 (1985) 3–31, has an excellent discussion of these sayings in their socio-economic setting of first-century Palestine. Matthew's interpretation, at least in practice, may have had the same restricted application to the immediate ecclesial setting that is reflected, for example, in the community discourse of ch. 18.

10. G. N. Stanton 'Aspects of Early Christian-Jewish Polemic and Apologetic' *NTS* 31 (1985) 377–392, especially 386f., who shows that a pattern of Sin, Exile, Return is to be found in a number of early Christian writings, including Matthew, which can juxtapose a harsh judgment on the Jewish leaders with an expression of hope in their future salvation, without any sense of contradiction.

Hans-Josef Klauck

Internal opponents: the Treatment of the Secessionists in the First Epistle of John

'THIS IS the victory that overcomes the world, our faith', it says in 1 John 5:4. Was this victory preceded by a battle? Are there those who are vanquished—those who have fallen to be lamented? What happened to those who were defeated? Were they sacrificed to the war-god of the victors? This kind of admittedly exaggerated question is provoked by the martial language of this verse. The aim of this article is to deal with the factual concerns hidden behind this language by seeking first of all to clarify the situation, then to investigate how the secessionists understood themselves, third to examine the counter-strategies and polemic of the author of the epistle, and finally to venture a critical evaluation.[1]

1. THE SITUATION

(a) The Johannine schism

The firm foundation for throwing light on the situation of the letter is provided by 1 John 2:19: 'They went out from us, but they were not of us; for if they had been of us, they would have continued with us; but they went out, that it might be plain that they all are not of us.'[2] The first impression evoked by the choice of words (cf. Deut. 13:13–14) suggests that a small heretical group has removed itself, possibly even through emigration in the geographical sense. But this impression reflects only the evaluation of the epistle's author: it does not correspond unconditionally to reality.[3] We can envisage the actual situation as follows. Disputes within the Johannine community of congregations over right doctrine and right practice have led to an irreparable split. The remnant centre on the epistle's author sees itself divided from the other section by an unbridgeable gap. Possibly it was numerically inferior, possibly the others commanded greater respect and chalked up more successes (see my comments below on 1 John 4:5). A formal excommunication of these opponents had not taken place: for this the conditions and means were lacking. The secessionists would have gone on living undisturbed as hitherto and would have felt themselves to be the true Johannine community. To them the writer of the epistle and his followers might seem to be a splinter group some of whom could still be brought over into their own camp (1 John 4:1 in combination with 2 John 7:10 takes into account the fact that the opponents' missionaries are active, even within the circle of those whom the author of the epistle is addressing).

The fact that this schism was preceded by a longer phase of the different groups co-existing within one and the same community is implicitly presupposed in 1 John 2:19 by the fourfold use of ἐξ ἡμῶν, 'from us', 'from among us'. In 1 John the preposition ἐκ, 'out of', 'from', expresses origin and belonging. It points to a preceding shared history.

(b) The social dynamics

A not inessential contribution to the intensification of the conflict was made by the social dynamics contained within it. This time let us begin with 1 John 4:5 'They [the opponents] are of the world, therefore what they say is of the world, and the world listens to them' (cf. John 3:31). What is to be gathered from this is that the secessionists were more successful in coming to terms with the non-Christian world in which they lived. In distinction from the remnant around the author of the epistle (cf. his emotional complaint in 1 John 4:6) they were able to attract attention, to gain a hearing for their message and possible even to acquire new members.

On this basis the warning in 1 John 2:15–17 against being conformed to the world is obviously to be seen against the background of the social situation and social conflicts. The list of vices in 1 John 2:16—especially with its mention of 'the pride of life', 'boasting about being well off', the last of the group of three—denounces the relationship between the opponents and their material possessions. Another passage that fits into this perspective is 1 John 3:17: 'But if any one has the world's goods and sees his brother in need, yet closes his heart against him, how does God's love abide in him?' The social divisions of the ancient world have left their traces even in the Johannine community. There were those who were better placed and there were those who were in need. The influential and well-off are probably to be sought particularly among the opponents of the epistle's author. Before the split they were from a material point of view very important for the community. They provided the rooms where they met, for example, they looked after the provision of food, they received with hospitality the travelling Johannine missionaries (cf. John 13:20, 3 John 5–8) and helped them too in many ways. With the break that was suddenly all in the past. The author of the epistle and his supporters suddenly find themselves confronted with financial problems they had not dreamed of. They feel themselves to be 'betrayed and sold'.

2. HOW THE OPPONENTS UNDERSTOOD THEMSELVES

Who were these secessionists and what were the fundamental convictions on the basis of which they tried to shape their lives as Christians? What from their point of view was the cause for the violent dispute with its schismatic consequences? The methodological problems that make it difficult to answer these questions are obvious. To begin with we have only the caricature which the author of the epistle sketched of them and which with the best will in the world one cannot classify as an objective evaluation of their concerns. Alongside this scholars have attempted to give the opponents' theology more definition by using the categories of the history of religion. Concepts like *gnosis* and 'docetism' regularly crop up in the relevant literature. It must be admitted that many features in the portrait of the opponents in 1 John tend to point in this direction. But this kind of labelling can lead very quickly to the individual peculiarities of this group being levelled out, quite apart from the fact that in their developed form gnosis and docetism are to be given a later date than the conflict reflected in 1 John (it is difficult to fix the date of the epistle later than about 100 AD). No attempt will therefore be made in what follows to use the history of religion to place the secessionists of 1 John: we shall limit ourselves to the data provided by the text.[4]

All the same in many passages the author of the epistle summarises his opponents' positions by brief references, as in 1:6, 8, 10; 2:4, 6, 9; 4:20; and indirectly in 3:2; 4:2–3; 5:6; and elsewhere. A closer examination and evaluation of the different pieces of evidence leads to the following picture. The opponents were marked by a strong and intense experience of the Spirit which however did not express itself in ecstatic phenomena but in a consistent and far-reaching internationalisation of the life of faith. They boasted of their knowledge of God, their fellowship with God, and their vision of God. Their eschatology bore an almost exclusively here and now character. For Christians they claimed sinlessness and did so from baptism. In general baptism played a great role in their thinking as the moment of receiving the Spirit and of changing one's life. This line was pursued as far as Christology. For the opponents the fundamental Christological fact was Jesus's baptism, at which according to John 1:32 the Spirit descended on him and remained with him so that he could now be called the 'Son of God' (John 1:34). To the same extent the incarnation and death on the Cross in their Christological and soteriological relevance retreated more and more into the background.

To all appearances these views were developed on the basis of the gospel according to St John in its original version before it was edited.[5] Above all certain texts in this gospel offer a suitable point of departure for the here and now eschatology but also for the evaluation of baptism as birth 'from above' (cf. John 3:5, 8), for regarding those who believed as being born of God (cf. John 1:12–13), and for other components of this way of thinking. The fact that the author of 1 John is basing himself on the same traditions has among other things the consequence that for the 'neutral' observer his position can hardly be distinguished from that of his opponents on many points (for example on the question of the sinlessness of those who believe, cf. 1 John 3:9) or the distinction becomes a matter of nuance.

3. THE COUNTER-STRATEGIES AND POLEMIC OF THE AUTHOR OF THE EPISTLE

(a) The theological counter-strategies

The dispute thus centres on the joint Johannine heritage and how it should be maintained, continued and developed. Here the author of 1 John develops a series of considerations which deserve complete respect as an attempt to come to grips with the theological situation.

A favourite expression of the author with which he begins his letter in 1 John 1:1 runs: ἀπ' ἀρχῆς, 'from the beginning'. Unmistakeably he is in this led by the endeavour to take from this beginning the moment beyond time that is attached to it in the gospel in John 1:1 and to link it back to key points within history. In 1 John 1:1 with 'that which was from the beginning' he was able to aim at the gradual process of Jesus's revelation of himself and the first disciples' corresponding realisation of this in the gospel (cf. John 2:11, 15:27). In the prologue to the letter (1 John 1:1–4) this enables him to allow the first witnesses, with whom he sees himself standing in a continuum of tradition mediated through the Johannine school, to speak in the first person. Otherwise in 1 John we encounter another use of ἀπ ἀρχῆς which has to do with the individual faith-history of Johannine Christians (if for the moment we disregard 2:13–14, which in my view is to be interpreted like 1:1, and 3:8). With this formula the author directs his readers' attention to the contents of the faith that were entrusted to them 'from the beginning', that is at baptism and during the instruction that preceded and followed it (1 John 2:7, 24; 3:11). The link that binds the different usages of ἀπ' ἀρχῆς is provided by the history of the Johannine community or 'Church history' which for the author of the letter begins with Jesus.

The conscious reference to the beginning also allows the author to give prominence to other old community traditions which had not found their way into the gospel and which were therefore ignored by the opponents. The first thing to be mentioned here is eschatology, which in 1 John in addition to its consistent here and now basis once again is given a more traditional orientation towards the future. This can be very well recognised in 1 John 3:1–2. The author of the epistle does indeed emphasise that those who believe are already now children of God, which is not something that can be taken for granted (cf. for example the use of the future in Matt. 5:9). But he adds at once that there is something essential still to come, being like God through seeing him, which he reserves for the *eschaton* in the strict sense. To these statements of the future belongs in addition the prospect of Christ's second coming which is still awaited (2:28) with the last judgement, as well as the use made of the figure known from Jewish and primeval Christian apocalyptic of an eschatological adversary of God or his anointed who is first given the name 'Antichrist' in 1 John (2:18, 22; 4:3)—an extremely significant event from the point of view of the history of effective action.

Slight shifts in comparison with the gospel are also to be observed with regard to the use of formulae expressing immanence like 'to be in', 'to remain in'. The letter applies these predominantly to God, not Christ (cf. especially 4:16). This new evaluation would have been suggested to the author by the opponents. Beyond this he prefers μένειν ἐν, 'to remain in', to εἶναι ἐν, 'to be in'. 'To remain' contains more strongly the temporal factor of staying, of lasting, of stability in mutual relationships. As an interpretation of the gospel's statements about immanence the author introduces the concept of κοινωνία, 'fellowship', a concept that is lacking in the gospel. 'Fellowship possesses an ecclesiological component that is lacking in the one-dimensionally conceived formulae of immanence. In the context this is shown by fellowship with God (1:6) having for the letter's recipients fellowship with those who embody the Johannine tradition as a condition (1:13), as is clear from the prologue to the letter. For the author of the epistle contingent forms of transmission necessarily arise from the historical contingency of the event of revelation in the human being Jesus of Nazareth. If one considers only 1:14 the impression appears of an early catholic conception of the transmission of tradition and of the understanding of ministry. It is understandable if earlier Catholic exegetes had difficulty in disguising the triumph in their voices when they came to interpret the prologue to the epistle,[6] but they are too quick to rejoice. They usually land in great difficulties when they have to explain 1 John 2:27. And there is more to be said.

In the centre of the dispute the author in 2:22–23 places acknowledgement of Jesus as Christ and Son of God. To be deduced from 4:2 is the more precise definition that for him it is indispensable, that Jesus as the Christ has come in the flesh, while 5:6 adds the coming in the blood that points to the death on the Cross. The protective framework around this confession of faith is formed by the Spirit and tradition, for according to 2:20–21 the gift of the Spirit offers all believers the best protection against being threatened by any form of false teaching, and in 2:24 the traditions of the beginning take over this protective role.

But what happens if the Spirit and tradition enter into competition with each other? The author does not seem to want to admit this possibility that actually occurred in practice: he is guided by the model of the paraclete from the farewell speech of the gospel where the opposition of Spirit and tradition seems transcended in a higher unity (cf. John 16:13–15). Other early Christian outlines bring another element into play in this place. They ascribe to the Church's ministry the task of securing the tradition and combating erroneous doctrine. It is remarkable that the author of the epistle actually rejects this possibility in 2:27: 'You have no need that any one should teach you.' That is meant in as fundamental a sense as it sounds. The author does not let himself be put off this programmatic attitude, which in true Johannine style trusts in the entire community in all its individual members being led by the Spirit, even by the occurrence of a schism which would seem rather to demand a firm hand.[7]

What should in no way be overlooked is that alongside these systematic discussions there is also a practical point of view which carries at least the same weight: the realisation of brotherly love or, as we would put it rather, love between brothers and sisters. The author does not tire of hammering home the commandment to love one another that is both new and old, and has three successive attempts at doing so to form a kind of crescendo (2:7–11, 3:11–24, 4:7–5:3); and he insists on its being put into practice. In this field he establishes the existence among his oponents of measurable deficiencies which in fact, as shown above, belong to the social consequences of the theological conflict. The question is merely—and here we make a transition to a more critical point of view—whether this love for one's brothers and sisters in the remnant that remains of the Johannine community does not signify a narrowing of the synoptic commandment to love one's neighbours and one's enemies. Does it not explicitly or implicitly exclude outsiders, non-Christians, and above all the opponents within the community? Are the boundaries of love therefore identical with the boundaries of one's own group? Sweeping statements are as little help here as anywhere, but one cannot easily dispute that this kind of danger is at least beginning to loom as a threatening development.

Nevertheless one could on the whole agree with Josef Blank's summing up of the character of 1 John: 'Certainly what we have here is an apologia on the highest theological level, since it follows from the core of the gospel and betrays a very reliable feeling for the decisive differences of doctrine with their disastrous consequences'—if, only if there were not the author's excessive polemic, something which equally deserves to be labelled 'disastrous'.

(b) Polemic

Let us then come to those passages where the theological dispute is enveloped in undisguised polemic of unheard-of ferocity, and let us start once again with 2:19. The phrase: 'It might be plain that they all are not of us' denies the joint history which, as demonstrated by the phrase 'they went out from us', lies behind the groups that have quarrelled. It never existed in reality; it was only a deceptive sham. In their hearts, in their inner beings the dissenters were never genuine members of the community: that is how the author of the epistle tries to come to terms with the traumatic experience of separation. Here another of the writer's tactics is already lurking. Symbolic figures and entities from the gospel which have negative associations and which are distinguished by their consistent enmity towards Christ are associated in 1 John with the opponents within the community. The verse 2:19 provides a concealed comparison between the opponents and Judas, who in the gospel only apparently belongs to the Twelve but on his first appearance he is already dismissed as a devil (John 6:70–71), allows himself to become the tool of Satan and goes out into the night of unbelief (John 13:30—ἐξῆλθεν, like 1 John 2:19).[9] In another passage the opponents are linked to the cosmos that is hostile to God (1 John 4:5) or with the unbelieving Jews (see below).

Even the adoption of the apocalyptic and primitive Christian figure of the antagonist at the end of time is put completely to polemical use against the opponents. This is already indicated by the new coinage 'Anti-Christ' which refers to the Christological controversies. For the writer the opponents are because of their deviant Christology the many Antichrists who as a collective represent definitively the apocalyptic antagonist. At work in them is the spirit of Antichrist, the spirit of deception (4:3, 6), to be classified as an evil demonic spirit.

The opponents' defective readiness to help is compared by the writer without further ado to murder (3:15, 17), and for this he has to hand a biblical model (the only one he uses in his letter), Cain, the murderer of his brother, 'who was of the evil one' (3:12). This at once links up with 3:8, 10, where the writer contrasts the children of God and the children of the devil. In the gospel the reproach of being children of the devil is applied to the Jews (John 8:44: 'You are of your father the devil, and your will is to do your father's desires'). The author of the epistle applies this to his opponents and condemns them by turning them into devils. He has determinedly driven this process of demonising them to this pitch.

The language with which the polemic of 1 John is clothed is very fundamental, very dualist and very mythological. Must it in fact also be called predestinarian, in the sense that a certain group of people precisely because of their origin cannot be other than of the devil and are helplessly condemned to sin? The author of the epistle here moves dangerously close to a boundary but without making the step to a doctrine of pure predestination. An indication of this should be that the term 'born of the devil' (analogous to 'born of God' in 3:9 and elsewhere) is deliberately avoided. A further indication consists of the fact that the author tries to link the phenomenon of the diabolical in history to certain human actions, as for example the action of Cain. His opponents have honestly deserved this verdict that now affects them with immense force through their own decisions and modes of behaviour: they have not fallen victim to an unavoidable disaster.

Did practice have at least a little more friendly aspect than relentless theory? In actual practice did the author of the epistle leave his opponents in individual cases the way open to change and to reconciliation with the remnant? This is what one would hope, and the abstract possibility exists because there is an absence of absolute predestinarian statements. But nowhere is it said explicitly, and we are far removed from certainty in this awkward question. Realistically we must also assume the worst, that the author of the epistle was unmoved by seeing the secessionists finally lost.

4. EVALUATION

The fact that the way in which the author of 1 John handles his opponents cannot count as an example worthy of imitation for theological discourse and even for theological quarrels hardly requires comment. We recognise clearly the way in which the basic dualistic structure of Johannine theology here comes up against a boundary. When it has to grapple with the phenomenon of genuine or supposed lack of faith and resistance to the proclamation of Christ it tends, when viewed from a human point of view, to pitilessness. The author of 1 John knows only black and white: intermediate shades are foreign to him. We see too what a disastrous weight can be obtained by the use of mythological material like the expectation of the Antichrist and Satanology. More than once they obstruct the better insights of the epistle's author.

It is of course right that much can be made historically understandable if one considers the writer's situation. At work are laws of social psychology which even Christian groups can only with difficulty evade: the discovery and safeguarding of identity by a group whose existence is threatened almost necessarily goes hand in hand with highly developed internal communication and cutting oneself off from the outside world. It is above all those who are blamed for the crisis, who are particularly experienced as a threat, who are regarded with hatred. But what is our theological position in all this, especially with regard to the commandment of love—provided we do not inadmissably start off by hedging it around with limitations? And with regard to the message of God's universal love for all men and women and for the entire world—a message maintained in principle even by the Johannine writings (cf. John 3:16, 1 John 4:9, 14)?

It is not primarily a question of heaping this early Christian theologian (whom we have to thank for 1 John) with reproaches, nor on the other hand taking an apologetic line and finding excuses for him at any price. It is concerned with the factual question which is, and remains, ours too. I would like to put it this way: if faith and love come into conflict, must love necessarily fall by the wayside? Simply to put the question already means in fact answering it with 'no'. Certainly the alternative cannot be to sacrifice faith when necessary to love.[10] The precedence over faith accorded by 1 John 3:24 has a certain factual rightness, because it corresponds to the way in which God's love comes first. The phrase 'God is love' (1 John 4:16) has its roots in God's act of love in Jesus Christ, and this can only be grasped and apprehended in faith. It is only in this way that God's love stands a chance among men and women.

What would be needed—and clearly this would be immensely difficult—

would be to develop forms of dealing with dissenters without giving up one's own standpoint of faith and without betraying love, which (to quote actual examples) renounced such things as condemning one's opponents as in league with the devil or heretics and similar hostile actions. That is something that has happened but rarely in the course of the history of the Church and of theology, beginning in the days when our New Testament writings were emerging. The task is one that remains with us.

Translated by Robert Nowell

Notes

1. In general for what follows readers should refer to the commentaries, cf. especially R. E. Brown *The Epistles of John* (Anchor Bible 30) (Garden City, NY 1982); R. Schnackenburg *Die Johannesbriefe* (Herders Theologischer Kommentar NT XIII/3) (Freiburg-im-Breisgau⁷ 1984); K. Wengst *Der erste, zweite und dritte Brief des Johannes* (Ökumenischer Taschenbuch-Kommentar 16) (Gütersloh/Würzburg 1978). On the question of the opponents in particular cf. A. Wurm *Die Irrlehrer im ersten Johannes-brief* (Biblische Studien VIII/1) (Freiburg-im-Breisgau 1903); K. Wengst *Häresie und Orthodoxie im Spiegel des ersten Johannesbriefes* (Gütersloh, 1976); G.Ghiberti 'Ortodossia e eterodossia nelle lettere giovannee', in *Rivista Biblica Italiana* 30 (1982), pp 381–400 (with references to the literature); J. Blank 'Die Irrlehrer des ersten Johannesbriefes' in *Kairos* 26 (1984) pp. 166–193; J. Painter 'The "Opponents" in 1 John' in *New Testament Studies* 32 (1986) pp. 48–71.
2. For the justification of this translation of the final phrase (rather than the alternative 'that not all are from our midst') cf. R. Schnackenburg *op. cit.* p. 151.
3. As has been strikingly observed by E. Haenchen 'Neuere Literatur zu den Johannesbriefen' in his *Die Bibel und Wir. Gesammelte Aufsätze II* (Tübingen 1968), pp. 235–311, here pp. 273–274.
4. J. M. Lieu '"Authority to Become Children of God": A study of 1 John', in *Novum Testamentum* 23 (1981) pp. 210–228, remarks somewhat sweepingly but not without justification (pp. 227–228): 'To understand 1 John we must not go in pursuit of docetics or gnostics as the villains of the piece; they are closer to home, the stepbrothers or, to change the image, the distorted reflections of the author himself; and it is to him we must look to understand his letter'.
5. On this especially R. E. Brown *op. cit.* pp. 71–86, who nevertheless puts many emphases differently.
6. Cf. for example the otherwise very level-headed W. Estius *Commentarius in Epistolam ad Hebraeos et septem Catholicas nova editio* (Paris 1891) p. 665. On the question of 'early Catholicism' in 1 John in general see C. C. Black II 'The Johannine Epistles and the Question of Early Catholicism' in *Novum Testamentum* 28 (1986) pp. 131–158: he comes to the conclusion that to begin with the category 'early Catholicism' is wrongly chosen.

7. For more detail on this see H. J. Klauck 'Gemeinde ohne Amt? Erfahrungen mit der Kirche in den johanneischen Schriften' in *Biblische Zeitschrift* NF 29 (1985) pp. 193–220.

8. J. Blank *op. cit.* p. 177.

9. For further material on this see H. J. Klauck *Judas – ein Jünger des Herrn* (Quaestiones Disputatae 111) (Freiburg-im-Breisgau 1987) pp. 70–92.

10. As is known this was Feuerbach's solution, cf. E. Jüngel 'Gott ist Liebe. Zur Unterscheidung von Glaube und Liebe' in *Festschrift für Ernst Fuchs* (Tübingen 1973) pp. 193–202.

Adela Yarbro Collins

Oppression from Without: the Symbolisation of Rome as Evil in Early Christianity

THE AMBIGUITY of the early Christian attitude toward Rome is perhaps best expressed in chapters 12–13 of Paul's letter to the Romans. He does not mention the emperor or other Roman officials explicitly, but exhorts the Christians of Rome to be subject to the rulers and other governing authorities, because all authority is from God (13:1–7). The context for this obedience is set by the preceding admonition to 'bless those who persecute you' (12:14). This lofty ethical standard is motivated in part by the reminder that God will avenge the persecuted by punishing the persecutor (12:19)! The book of Acts ends with a portrayal of Paul proclaiming the kingdom of God and teaching about the Lord Jesus Christ openly and unhindered in the city of Rome. This positive ending overlooks, probably deliberately, the execution of Paul by the Roman authorities. A major theme in 1 Peter is that Christians, maintaining a righteous way of life, should accept suffering for the faith in imitation of the model provided by Jesus. Even this beautiful call to the purifying suffering of the innocent is reinforced by the reminder that those outside the household of God, the impious and the sinners, will be judged (4:17–18). Finally, 'Babylon', a symbol rich with negative connotations, is used as a code-name for Rome, where the author is depicted as residing (5:13).

This ambivalence in the early Christian attitude to Rome is due in part to the interaction of Christians with Roman authorities and in part to the

66

historical inheritance received by Christians from Jews. The early interaction of the Jews and the Romans was positive. In the second century, BCE, the Jews appreciated the Romans' initiatives in limiting the expansion of the Graeco-Syrian kingdom. One of these interventions is mentioned in Dan. 11:29–30, in which the Romans are called 'Kittim'. In his struggle to gain and maintain independence for the Jews from the Graeco-Syrian kingdom, Judas Maccabaeus sought and obtained the friendship and alliance of the Romans (1 Maccabees 8). In the Second Temple period Jews settled in many cities around the Mediterranean. In some cases they had settled in a city as colonists with the backing of a Hellenistic king. They thus had extensive civil rights and a political organisation of their own, although, for religious reasons, they were not citizens. The Roman authorities consistently protected and reaffirmed the civil rights of these Jews of the Dispersion. The attitude of many of the Jews of Judaea changed, however, when the Roman general Pompey conquered the region and brought it under Roman power in 63 BCE. He was said to have entered the most holy part of the Temple, entrance to which was restricted to the High Priest on the Day of Atonement. He thus was remembered as a brutal conqueror and perpetrator of sacrilege, for example, in the Psalms of Solomon, which were composed in the latter part of this first century BCE.

For a variety of reasons—religious, political, social, and economic—many Jews of the first century CE wished to throw off the yoke of the Romans and return to autonomous self-rule, preferably under an anointed king of the line of David. This desire led to the first Jewish war with Rome which lasted from 66 to 72 and resulted in the destruction of Jerusalem and the temple in 70. This was a catastrophe of major proportions. Some Jews, such as Josephus, thought that the revolt was a mistake and that the Romans were right in crushing it. Some Christians—for example the author of the gospel according to Matthew—believed that the event was a punishment decreed by God because the people of Jerusalem had rejected Jesus, God's Messiah (Matt. 22:1–10). Other Jews such as the author of an apocalypse attributed to Ezra (2 Esdras 3–14) assimilated Rome to the first destroyer of Jerusalem, Babylon, and believed that the Roman deed revealed the true character of the empire as wicked and ungodly (2 Esd. 12:31–32). One of the climactic visions of the book portrays Rome as a many-headed eagle which would be destroyed by a lion (the Messiah) at the end of days (2 Esd. 11–12).

Among some Jews, the Roman destruction of the Temple led to the expression of intense anti-Roman sentiments. Such expression begins with the Jewish redaction of Book 4 of the Sibylline Oracles, which dates to about 80 CE. It reaches a climax in Book 5 of the same collection, written between 70 and 130 CE. In Book 5, Rome is criticised for sexual immorality, for destroying Jerusalem, and for claiming divine honours. Nero, who was emperor at the beginning of the Jewish war, is portrayed as the eschatological adversary, modelled in part on the symbolic portrayal of Antiochus Epiphanes in the book of Daniel. The literary expression of anti – Roman feeling was accompanied by continuing political agitation, which led to the revolt in the Dispersion under Trajan in 115 and the second Jewish war in Judaea under Hadrian in 132.

The book of Revelation is the most, if not the only, anti-Roman text in the New Testament. The vehement anti-Roman propaganda found in the Jewish book 5 of the Sibylline Oracles and in the Christian book of Revelation reappears in the Christian book 8 of the Sibylline Oracles, which was written about 175 CE under Marcus Aurelius. Like Jewish apocalyptic literature, the book of Revelation refers to Rome under the code name 'Babylon' (14:8; 16:19; 17:5; 18:2, 20, 21). The use of this name is a clear allusion to the destruction of Jerusalem. The author's reaction to the event seems to be similar to that of the author of Matthew, since the historical Jerusalem is called 'allegorically' or 'spiritually': *Sodom* and *Egypt* (11:8). Nevertheless, Rome is the primary earthly enemy of God and the people of God.

The allusions to Rome are most clear in the second half of the work (chapters 12–22). Chapter 12 presents a great conflict between a heavenly woman and a great fiery dragon. The woman symbolises the people of God and the dragon, Satan. When the dragon is unable to seize the child of the woman or the woman herself, he goes off to make war on the rest of her offspring. His instrument in this war is a great beast which arises out of the sea (13:1). This beast recalls Leviathan of the Old Testament and the four beasts of Daniel 7—especially the fourth (note that the eagle of the apocalypse of Ezra is explicitly identified with the fourth kingdom of Daniel; 2 Esd. 12:11). This ancient symbol is adapted to symbolise the Roman empire. This is suggested by the statement that it was allowed to exercise power for 42 months (13:5). The same period of time is allotted to 'the nations' who trample the holy city (11:2). The connection is reinforced by the remarks that 'authority was given [the beast] over every tribe and people and tongue and nation' (13:7), a hyperbolic allusion to Rome's virtually universal rule, and that 'all who dwell on earth will worship [the beast]' (13:8), a reference to the widespread practice of giving divine honours to the Roman emperors and the goddess/city Roma. The end of the beast is described in chapter 19. After the battle between the Word of God with the armies of heaven and the beast with the kings of the earth, the beast is captured and thrown alive into the lake of fire (19:20).

Chapter 16 contains an account of the pouring out of the seven bowls and the plagues which follow. The result of the seventh bowl is, 'The great city was split into three parts, and the cities of the nations fell, and God remembered great Babylon, to make her drain the cup of the fury of his wrath' (16:19). This brief announcement is elaborated in the following chapter. The city is personified as a woman—a prostitute with whom the kings of the earth have prostituted themselves (17:1–2). She is clothed in purple and scarlet, adorned with gold, jewels, and pearls, and holds a golden cup (17:4). That the woman is Rome is indicated by the remark that she is seated on seven mountains or hills (17:9) and that she is the great city which has dominion over the kings of the earth (17:18). The vision suggests that Roma is not a goddess as the Romans and their political allies claim, but rather a prostitute, the mother of prostitutes and of the abominations of the earth (17:5).

The harlot is depicted as riding a beast with ten horns. The beast symbolises one of the emperors of Rome (17:10–11). The ten horns represent ten kings who will ally themselves with the beast (17:12–13). The horns and the beast 'will hate the prostitute; they will make her desolate and naked, and devour her flesh and burn her up with fire' (17:16). In this vision the Nero legend has been adapted to describe the events of the end time. Nero was once ruler of Rome. Because of opposition to him among the senatorial families of Rome, he was forced either to flee or to commit suicide. He chose to commit suicide, but the rumour arose that he had fled to the Parthians, a people of the East who were his friends. This rumour developed into a legend among the ordinary people of the eastern Mediterranean, for whom Nero was a kind of hero. It involved his return from the East with Parthian armies and regaining power by conquering Rome in battle. Because of his moral failings, such as the murder of his mother, his desire for divine honours, and his involvement in the Jewish war, some eastern Jews inverted the Nero legend, so that he became a demonic being who would return from the ends of the earth to destroy Rome and thus, inadvertently, avenge Jerusalem (Sib. Or. 4.119–24, 138–39; Sib. Or. 5.137–54, 361–85). The author of Revelation seems to have incorporated the Jewish form of the legend in his scenario of the 'End Times'. He presents Nero as one who will return from the dead in a parody of Jesus' resurrection (13:3, 14; 17:8, 11). The main interest in chapter 17 is the destruction of the woman who symbolises Rome. Chapter 18 is an elaborate commentary on her (predicted) destruction given in dramatic form. The passage is framed by two announcements of judgment, each given by an angel. (18:1–3 and 21–24). Following an admonition to the people of God (18:4–8) are three scenes of mourning in which the friends of Rome, the kings of the earth, the merchants and the shipmasters and seafarers, weep and wail over her demise (18:9–19).

In light of these visions, one more allusion to Rome may be discerned. In the message to the congregation at Pergamum, their city is described as the place where Satan's throne is, the dwelling place of Satan (2:13). This depiction has been interpreted by some in terms of the presence of a shrine of Asclepios in Pergamum and by others with reference to the famous altar dedicated to Zeus. In light of chapters 12–13, it is more likely that Satan's influence is seen in terms of Roman power. The allusion may be to the fact that the Roman governor heard legal cases regularly in Pergamum. Antipas, who was killed for his witness to Christ, may have been tried by the governor.

It is clear that the strongest possible language is used in the book of Revelation to depict Rome in a negative light. In the message to Pergamum (2:13) and in the visions which open the second half of the book (chapters 12–13), Rome is associated with Satan. 'Satan' is a term which designated the 'accuser' in a legal situation. The name thus evokes the image of a heavenly court in which Satan accuses individual members of the people of God before the throne of God. The image of the heavenly court provides an interpretation of the earthly courts in which Christians, such as Antipas, are accused. Although they are convicted in the earthly court and lose their physical lives, they are acquitted in the heavenly court and victorious over Satan (12:10–11). The image of the serpentine dragon who sweeps down stars and spews water is an ancient symbol of chaos, of the forces which threaten creation and order (12:4, 15). The serpentine dragon is also the ancient serpent of Genesis 2–3, by the time of Revelation identified with the Devil, who deceived Adam and Eve (12:9). Through his agent, the beast from the earth, the Devil continues to deceive humanity with signs and wonders, which lead them to worship the Roman emperor as if he were a god (13:13–15). The Devil and his allies will deceive the kings of the inhabited world so that they assemble their armies for the final battle of Armageddon (cf. 20:3 with 16:13–14). The Devil's deceptions are temporarily ended by his confinement for the thousand years of the messianic kingdom (20:1–6). But when the thousand years are ended, he will be loosed and will proceed to deceive Gog and Magog and gather them for battle against the saints in Jerusalem (20:7–9). This final attack will be defeated by divine power and the Devil will join the beast in the lake of fire (20:9–10). The association of Rome with Satan links Rome to disobedience and moral evil through the allusion to the story of Adam and Eve. The primary connotation of the association, however, is one of struggle, power, and rebellion. The images for Satan's opposition to God and the people of

God include verbal attacks on the heavenly court, but are mainly violent images of physical attack and pitched battle (12:4, 7, 10, 13, 15; 16:14, 16; 20:7–10).

Similarly, the Roman empire as beast-like is depicted as a power which opposes God and attempts to usurp God's power and the honour due to God alone. The Leviathan-like character of 'the beast' calls to mind the theme of 'the Divine Warrior', doing battle to establish the created world (Ps. 74:12–17; cf. Isa. 51:9). Major aspects of the description of the beast are its blasphemous name (some divine epithet; 13:1) and its haughty and blasphemous words (claims to be invincible, eternal and thus divine: 13:5–6). The idolatry condemned in the passage, the worship of the beast by all the inhabitants of the earth (13:4, 8), is presented not only as a moral evil but also as a rebellion against God—an attempt to usurp the honour due to God alone.

In chapter 17 and especially chapter 18, reasons are given for the punishment of Rome. These reasons may also be seen as explanations for the literary process of the dehumanisation and demonisation of Rome. The most explicit and defensible reason is the violence for which Rome is responsible. The prostitute is portrayed as drunk with the blood of the saints and the witnesses of Jesus (17:6). When she is slain, 'in her was found the blood of prophets and saints, and of all who have been slain on the earth' (18:24). Here the text expresses concern not only for the self-interest of its intended readers or hearers, but for all the oppressed of the earth. Similarly, there is a hint that Rome is condemned in part for the slave trade in which her merchants engaged (18:!3). Another reason for judgment is Rome's deluded sense of its invulnerability, a confidence which forgets human weakness and dependence on God (18:7–8). The image of prostitution in these chapters is ambiguous. It probably alludes both to the great wealth of the leading Roman citizens and their allies as well as to the divine honours given to Rome. In the latter case, the image of prostitution echoes the admonitions of the prophets of Israel in which they compared the idolatry of the people to fornication, adultery, and prostitution. The implied condemnation of Roman wealth probably reflects a sense of injustice at the wide disparity between rich and poor in the Roman empire at the end of the first century CE.

Even though one may be persuaded that there were grounds for a strident prophetic critique of Rome when Revelation was written, one is struck, not only by the dehumanisation of the enemy through the choice of images, but also at the expressed attitude of the oppressed toward the oppressor. The souls of those who had been slain for the word of God and for the witness they had borne are not depicted as loving their enemies, as forgiving them, or as praying for their conversion, but as calling out to God to avenge their blood (6:9–11). The angel over the waters does not provide the readers with an example of turning the other cheek, but rather of 'an eye for an eye and a tooth for a tooth'. Those who have shed the blood of saints and prophets will be given blood to drink, for 'They deserve it!' (16:4–7). The image of the prostitute being made desolate and naked, having her flesh devoured and burned up with fire, is a violent one, which under most circumstances would evoke pity. Yet God is presented as putting this deed into the hearts of its perpetrators so that they might carry out God's purpose (17:17).

Chapter 18 is very effective dramatically. It begins with an announcement of judgment and an admonition which justify the horrible fate predicted for Rome (18:1–8). It moves into scenes of mourning and pathos, as the friends of Rome bewail the end of her glory. These scenes evoke a certain empathy and pity for Rome on the part of the reader or hearer, in spite of the overall context in which Rome is presented as enemy. So the abrupt shift from mourning to rejoicing is a shock: 'In one hour she has been laid waste. Rejoice over her, O heaven, O saints and apostles and prophets, for God has given judgment for you against her!' (18:19–20). A final announcement of judgment which is both sad and judgmental follows (18:21–24) and then comes an extended scene of heavenly rejoicing over the fall of Babylon, which is depicted as the victory of God (19:1–8). The scene proclaims justice. 'for [God's] judgments are true and just; he has judged the great prostitute who corrupted the earth with her prostitution, and he has avenged on her the blood of his servants' (19:2), but there is no encouragement to love one's enemies. On the contrary, the emotional impact of the scene is to encourage joy over the imagined punishment of one's enemies: 'Once more they cried, "Hallelujah! The smoke from her goes up for ever and ever".' (19:3).

Also in chapter 19 is an account of the final battle alluded to in 14:14–20, 16:12–16, and 17:14, in which the Messiah/Lamb/Word of God defeats the beast and its allies, including all the kings of the earth and their armies. It is possible to read this account, not as an actual battle, but as an unbloody victory of Christ, in which the sword of his mouth is understood as his word (compare 2 Esd. 13:25–38). But the language evokes a long tradition of Holy War, in which God's victory is won through violence and the earth is fertilised by blood (cf. Isa. 34:1–7). The text emphasises, not only that the leaders, the beast from the sea and the beast from the earth (the false prophet), will be cast into the lake of fire, but also that 'the rest were slain by the sword of him who sits on the horse'. The 'banquet' of the vultures which follows is truly grisly. The scavengers are called 'to eat the flesh of kings, the flesh of captains, the flesh of mighty men, the flesh of horses, and their riders, and the flesh of all men, both free and slave, both small and great' (19:18). The vision concludes with the remark, 'and all the birds were gorged with their flesh' (19:21).

The sifting of the sheep from the goats continues right to the end of the book. At the final judgment, all those whose names are not found in the Book of Life will be thrown into the lake of fire (20:15). In the vision of the new creation. God is introduced with tender and comforting words (21:3–4). The actual speech of God which is presented in 21:5–8 begins with promises, but ends with a threat. 'But as for the cowardly, the faithless, the polluted, as for murderers, prostitutes, sorcerers, idolaters, and all liars, their lot shall be in the lake that burns with fire and sulphur, which is the second death.' One of the concluding prophetic sayings announces that 'Outside [the new Jerusalem] are the dogs and sorcerers and prostitutes and murderers and idolaters, and every one who loves and practises falsehood' (22:15). These statements may be interpreted as admonitions to the faithful to remain faithful. The admonition of 14:12 seems to give such a connotation to the threat of 14:9–11. Nevertheless, the contrast between the faithless and the faithful (note 21:7 in contrast to 21:8 and 22:14 to 22:15) impresses upon the reader or hearer the notion that all humanity is divided into two groups, the insiders and the outsiders, and that the outsiders are already condemned. Consider the remark in 22:11, 'Let the evildoer still do evil, and the filthy still be filthy, and the righteous still do right, and the holy still be holy.'

This dualism of insiders and outsiders is part of the larger dualistic thought-world of Revelation in which all living creatures are placed. At the pinnacle of power on one side is God, the ruler of all (1:8). On the other is Satan, who has power, a throne and great authority (13:2). Allied with God is the Lamb who was slain (5:6). Allied with Satan is the beast from the sea (13:1–2). All the people of the earth are divided into two groups, those who have the seal of God on their foreheads and whose names are in the book of life (3:5, 12; 7:3; 20:4; 21:27; 22:4) and those who bear the mark of the beast and worship it (9:4; 13:8, 17; 14:9–11; 16:2; 20:15). This literary tension reflects the political tension between the adherents of the kingdom of God and those of the kingdom of Caesar (11:15: 12:10; 16:10; 17:18). The literary tension reflects a tension in the experience of the author and his audience between social experience and faith. They believed that God and his anointed were the rulers of the world and that those who believed in them shared their autonomy and power. Their social experience contradicted that faith, in that they were economically disadvantaged, socially harassed, and politically in danger of denunciation and execution. The narrative of the book of Revelation is a literary attempt to overcome this tension by showing that God and Christ are truly in power now and that this power will be manifested fully in the future.

The dehumanising, demonising, and violent language of Revelation may be seen as aiding in the process of overcoming social tension in two ways. First, it may be seen as part of a process of containing aggressive feelings. Given the superior power of Rome in the first century, it was more practical to imagine the destruction of Rome than to take up arms and rebel. Such an imaginative way of dealing with aggressive feelings is also morally superior to acting them out in violent deeds. The book of Revelation contains violent images, but it does not encourage its audience to engage in violent activity. Second, the portrayal of the enemy as sub-human and demonic and the prediction of the enemy's downfall served to define Christian identity over against Graeco-Roman culture. It helped to establish boundaries between Christian social groups and other voluntary associations of the time. Such a setting of boundaries was important in order to guard against syncretism and assimilation which may have resulted in the loss of any distinctive Christian message and life-style. Such a process preserves the religious value of monotheism and rejects idolatry.

The solution of Revelation, however, was unstable. Even though violent activity is not encouraged by the text, the use of violent imagery may lead to the eruption of violence at any time. The aggressive feelings are contained only, not eliminated. The desire for vengeance upon one's enemies falls short of the highest levels of Jewish and Christian ethical teaching. One does not find anything in Revelation like Ezra's concern for the multitudes which will be damned (2 Esd. 7:45–48, 62–69). Likewise, the spirit of the Sermon on the Mount is lacking, in which the followers of Jesus are called to avoid not only murder, but also anger (Matt. 5:21–26). The setting of firm boundaries over against those with whom one differs carries within it the seeds of endless schism within the new group itself. The messages seem to reflect the beginnings of such schisms (2:6, 14–15, 20–25).

The book of Revelation too easily supports a literalistic reading of the early Christian proverb, 'The first shall be last and the last shall be first'. In reading and applying the book of Revelation today, the interpreter should reflect, 'What does it profit the oppressed to become the oppressor?'

Christopher Rowland

Keeping Alive the Dangerous Vision of a World of Peace and Justice

HOPE EXISTS for the sake of the hopeless. . . . All memory of suffering awakens dangerous visions, visions that are dangerous for those who try to control the present or the future. They are visions of the kingdom of justice, which enable the suffering people to shake off their bonds and to keep moving along the road to liberation.[1]

1. THE SEARCH FOR CHRISTIAN MESSIANISM

Christianity began life as part and parcel of second Temple Judaism, but it rapidly became a very different religion, whose concerns can be linked with its Jewish antecedents, yet has moved far from those original concerns with obedience to the Torah which characterise life of the convenant people. Nowhere is this difference expressed more clearly than in the realm of messianism and eschatology. Christianity repudiated the hope of the reign of God on earth and instead looked for the fulfilment of the divine promises in a transcendent realm. Similarly it is often asserted that the political messianism of Judaism was rejected in favour of a non-violent 'spiritual' messianism. In the process chilastic beliefs were repudiated or reinterpreted. It is one of the features of twentieth century theology that eschatology and politics have had a wedge driven between them because of the abandonment of the chiliastic/millenarian tradition by Christian theology, and thereby the this-worldly messianism which is the most important legacy of the

Jewish scriptures. Part of the task of bibilical interpretations is to transcend the damaging dualism between eschatological and political theology and so cement the link with Judaism and the world of injustice which demands messianic praxis here and now.[2]

2. TRANSFORMING MESSIANISM

Two features of early Christianity have continued to fascinate me. Firstly, there is the way in which a movement which was so firmly based in a Jewish matrix should have become overtly theological in its extant writings when the parent religion was moving (and, in my view, was already in the period of the Second Temple firmly attached) to the priority of the ethical in its understanding of religion. Secondly, by the end of the second century the messianic and millenarian elements which Christianity had inherited from Judaism were in the process of being marginalised or domesticated. Accommodation with the existing order and a growing concentration on theology and the life of the ecclesia was matched by a diminution of interest in the expectation of a coming reign of the messiah on earth. Of course, eschatological ideal persisted within the early Church, particularly among groups which were marginalised by the emerging dominant ideology. It is no surprise, therefore, that by the fourth century Eusebius of Caesarea was speaking in a disparaging way of the chiliasm of Papias of Hierapolis, though neglecting to mention that other theological giants of the second half of the second century—like Justin and Irenaeus—were likewise committed to such views.

The messianic group could erupt from the seething cauldron of an expectant society, develop its beliefs and practices and indeed find itself at odds with those outside its circle (as the nascent Christian movement certainly did). If it survived, the heady enthusiasm which characterises the initial outburst evolved prompted by disappointment or the need for consolidation and accommodation. Also, when a messianism moved to different settings and into different social strata, there was bound to be an effect of the socio-economic reality on those ideas. One of the fascinating things about the formation of ideologies is the subtle way in which language can undergo significant shifts of meaning in different social contexts.[3] The radical political thrust of millenarian beliefs means that rapid shifts in the core meaning of dominant ideas can take place, and then they can be accommodated into a dominant ideology with their cutting edge blunted.

One of the features of messianism is that it represents a clear alternative to conventional wisdom and custom. What is more, its adherents frequently regard their beliefs as matters for present implementation rather than pious platitudes relating to some uncertain future. It is precisely that energy which enables the millennial beliefs to transform existence which makes them such a disruptive force within society and elicits a violent reaction either from without or, more often, from within the movement itself. To be part of a messianic movement means to be part of social change, almost certainly of an unpredictable form. However well mapped out the received wisdom on the future hope may have been, the challenge of claims to fulfilment to that system of beliefs inevitably leads to new responses which push the adherents along an uncharted path of religious and social experiment. There is usually little guidance. Indeed, if the Jewish material now extant is anything to go by, primitive Christians who believed that a new order had dawned with Jesus, had little information to go on as they set out to explore the implications of what they were doing and saying for the culture of which they were a part.

In this respect the book of revelation is a classic messianic text which its uncompromising dualism and negative assessment of the injustice of the ruling power and its spurious claim to recognition. As such it stands in the sharpest possible contrast with those strands within Christianity which sought continuity with the world as it was and found value in its ideas and institutions. What is most important for the debate between Church and synagogue was that it kept alive the need for a critical distance from contemporary culture which Judaism had always maintained in the distinctiveness of its practice and its complete repudiation of idolatry. So on the margins of the Christian canon Jewish messianism was preserved. Revelation so firmly demands that Christians remember that their canon contains two parts. Thus the New Testament must, as Paul Ricoueur has argued,[2] be regarded as the re-reading of the Jewish scriptures.

The book of Revelation has been the basis of the appeal for radical social and political change throughout the history of the Church, and it is no surprise that it should continue to be the seed-bed of revolutionary religious action in our generation. In this it presents a challenge to the Church to take seriously that Jewish inheritance as a necessary corrective to the temptation to the flight from history and the solid obligation to seek the justice of God in human affairs which the Hebrew scriptures demand of us.

3. APOCALYPSE: AN UNMASKING OF REALITY[4]

The New Testament Apocalypse sets out to reveal things as they really are —in both the life of the Christian communities and the world at large.

In so doing it gives little comfort to the complacent Church or the powerful world. For the powerful and the complacent it has a message of judgment and doom, whereas for the powerless and oppressed it offers hope and vindication. The characterisation of contemporary society in the apocalyptic symbolism of 'beast' and 'harlot' is a vigorous unmasking and denuciation of the ideology of the powerful, by which they seek to legitimise their position by persecution and economic exploitation; it is an ancient Christian form of the critique of ideology. The critique of the present is effected by the use of a contrast between the glories of the future and the inadequacies of the present. The process of unmasking involves an attempt not only to delineate the true character of contemporary society and the super-human forces at work in the opposition to God's righteousness in the world. Also, the enormous power of those forces which undergird the oppression and unrighteousness of the world order are shown to be unstable and destined to defeat. In contrast the apparent fragility of the witness of those who follow the way of Jesus is promised ultimate vindication.

Revelation is not a detailed blueprint of an ideal society to be contemplated at leisure or which engages the reader only temporarily. Hope inspires action, readiness to suffer, and urgent need of repentance in the face of catastrophe. It seeks to persuade its readers that the present moment is a time of critical importance. The outline of future history is offered as the basis for a change of heart to engage the whole of life in its drama which will have drastic consequence for the one who reads it. Acceptance or rejection of its message is nothing less than the difference between alignment with the reign of God which is to come or sharing the fate of the 'beast' in the Lake of Fire.

4. THE RESOLUTION OF THE SOCIAL CONTRADICTIONS OF THE PRESENT IN THE VISION OF THE NEW CREATION

Revelation offers canonical justification for the cosmic and historical context of divine activity. The view, so deeply imbedded in the Jewish scriptures, was subordinated in mainstream Christian doctrine to the concern for the individual soul, a process already evident in the New Testament. The struggle between darkness and light in human affairs was neglected in favour of that conflict in the human heart. The Book of Revelation has provided encouragement for all those who look for the fulfilment of God's righteousness in human history.

The contrast between the vision of the new Jerusalem in ch. 21 with the initial vision of the heavenly court in ch. 4 also should be noted. In Rev. 4

the seer is granted a glimpse into the environs of God. Here God the Creator and Liberator is acknowledged, and, as we notice from the following chapter, it is from the God of the universe that the historical process beings which leads to the establishment of a new aeon after the manifestation of divine judgment. In the chapters following (4–5) we find the picture of a world afflicted but unrepentant—indeed, manifesting precisely the kind of misguided devotion to evil which has to be rooted out before God's kingdom can finally come. In Rev. 4ff. God is still in heaven, and it is there that the heavenly host sing his praise and magnify his name. There is a contrast with Rev. 21 where God's dwelling is on earth; it is no longer in heaven.

This contrast between heaven and earth disappears in the new creation. Now the tabernacling of God is with humanity, and they shall be his people. God's dwelling is not to be found above the cherubim in heaven; for God's throne is set right in the midst of the New Jerusalem where the living waters stream from the throne and God's servants marked with the mark of God will see God face to face. Here we have an example of theological immanentism which is predicted for the New Age. It is only then that there will be the conditions for God and humanity to dwell in the harmony which was impossible while there was rejection of the divine righteousness in human affairs. Heaven on earth is what the new age is all about. God is no longer transcendent but immediate—part and parcel of that world of perfection and evident in it. Indeed, those who are his will be his children and carry his name on their heads: they will be identified with the character of God and enjoy God's presence unmediated. In the apocalyptic vision, therefore, the contradictions of a fractured existence are resolved in the harmony offered by the apocalyptic text. Apocalyptic writers were convinced that this divine immanence was not reserved solely for the New age. The glory which the apocalyptic seer enjoyed in his revelation was a matter of living experience here and now for those who confessed Jesus as messiah and participated in the eschatological spirit. Already those who possessed the spirit of God were sons and daughters of God; already those in Christ were a new creation and a Temple of the divine spirit. That hope for the final resolution of the contrast between heaven and earth was already perceived by those who had eyes to see and know it.

5. EPISTLE AND APOCALYPSE

(a) Concentrating the Mind on the Reality which confronts the Reader

The Apocalypse can remind readers of early Christian literature that the hope for a reign of God on earth, when injustice and oppression will be swept away and the structures of an evil society broken down, is an important component of the Christian Gospel. It is easy to imagine how easy it would have been for the early Christians to have capitulated to their feelings of political powerlessness by concentrating on individual holiness only. But Paul, for example, speaks of a process of salvation which is firmly rooted in the process of libertion for the whole of creation. similarly, the Apocalypse does not easily allow a retreat into the conventicle as the main arena of divine activity, for it persuades the saints to prophesy before the world about the righteousness of God and the dreadful consequences of ignoring its implementation.

The readers of the Apocalypse are not allowed to dream about millennial bliss without being brought face to face with the obstacles which stand in the way of its fulfilment and the costly part to be played by them in that process. One of the problems of utopianism is that it can lead the reader in to construction of ideal worlds which distract him or her from the demands of the present. Those demands are evident in 'the letters to the churches' which introduce the vision of hope and in the concluding admonitions which stress the authority of the text and the imminence of the fulfilment of its message. Utopianism can lead to an escape from reality however much its attempts betoken that yearning for something better. Writers who resort to utopianism do so as a compensation for the inability to do anything about the world as it is. The book of Revelation offers a timely reminder in its own form about supposing that its preoccupation with eschatological matters offers an opportunity to avoid the more challenging preoccupations of the present. Thus, the vision of hope inaugurated by the exaltation of the Lamb is set within the framework of the 'letters of the seven churches'. The promise of a part in the New Jerusalem is linked with present behaviour. The readers of the Apocalypse are not allowed to dream about millennial bliss without being brought face to face with the obstacles which stand in the way of its fulfilment and the costly part to be played by them in that process: they have to wash their robes and make them white in the blood of the Lamb, and avoid being marked with the mark of the beast?

Similarly in the Marcan eschatological discourse the preoccupation of the bulk of the material is not so much the satisfaction of curiosity about the details of the times and seasons so much as dire warnings of the threat of being led astray, of failing at the last and of the need to be ready and watchful to avoid the worst of the disasters which are to come. In the bleak moments of the last days in Jerusalem there is little attempt to dwell on the privileges of discipleship (though an eschatological promise is made to the disciples a little later in the Lucan story in Luke 22:29f. in the context of the

Supper discourse). It is not a future without hope but the thoughts of the hearers are made to dwell on responsibilities in the short and medium term as the essential prerequisite of achieving an millennial bliss. There is in fact very little attempt made to sketch the character of the liberation which draws near. The sketch of the ideal society or the ideal world is lacking, a mark of either a lack of any political realism or of a merely utopian fixation.

The certainty of vindication is there but the lot of the elect when they have been gathered from the four corners of the earth is not touched on at all in Mark. The element of judgment at the Parousia of the Son of Man is not entirely absent, however, from the synoptic discourses as the climax of the Matthean version is the account of the final assize with the Son of Man sitting on God's throne separating the sheep from the goats. But here as elsewhere in these discourses the focus of attention is on the present response of the elect. It is the recognition of the heavenly Son of Man in the brethren who are hungry, thirsty, strangers, naked, weak and imprisoned in the present age who will inherit the kingdom prepared by God from the foundation of the world.

The eschatological discourse in the synoptic gospels must not be separated from the narrative of Jesus' proclamation and inauguration of the reign of God. It is that context which is necessary to prevent the discourse about the future becoming the goal of the narrative. Discipleship involves sharing the way of the Cross of the Son of Man as he goes up to Jerusalem. What is offered the disciple is the sharing of the cup of suffering of the Son of Man rather than the promise of sitting at his right hand and his left when he reigns on earth. It is not that this request is repudiated but, as the eschatological discourse makes plain, there can be no escape from the painful reality of the present witness with its need to endure the tribulations which precede the vindication. That is the challenge which faces those who wish to live out the messianic narrative in their own lives; no short cuts to the messianic reign are to be found here. It is easy to see how the discourse material in the gospels can be extracted from their narrative context and function as instructions which abstract the reader from the challenge of the messianic way as it intersects with an order which is passing away.

(b) Epistle and Apocalypse: the scope of Christian Concern

Those letters reflect the ambiguities and contradictions of life. Even the most overtly messianic and historically oriented text of the New Testament cannot but be affected by the contradictions between hope and improverished reality. The letters which impress on readers the importance of present action indicate a degree of interest in specifically religious issues, (one of the reasons, one suspects, that these letters continue to gain a more ready hearing from contemporary Christian audiences). That concern to recapture one's first one love and endeavour to maintain the purity of relationship to the lord who stands in the midst of his churches (1:19) indicates the emerging preoccupation with personal and ecclesial holiness which is itself part of the reaction to political impotence. The letter, that medium of the Pauline urban Christianity which appears so different from the world of Jesus and the first followers of Jesus (to borrow Gerd Theissen's description) seems also to embody that spirit of urban Christianity, where accommodation with the surrounding culture and acceptance of its priorities are a greater issue.

6. KEEPING ALIVE THE OPPRESSED CULTURE IN THE FACE OF A DOMINANT IDEOLOGY

The role of the follower of the messiah is not quiet resignation. In the unfolding eschatological drama in the main body of the Apocalypse the involvement of the seer in chapter 10 when he is instructed to eat the scroll and commanded to prophesy is a direct call to participate actively as a prophet rather than merely be a passive spectator of it. Revelation is insistent that the role of the martyr or witness is of central importance. Jesus of Nazareth is the faithful prophetic witness, and his followers have to continue that testimony of Jesus. That will involve suffering in the great tribulation, but those who join the messianic throng are those 'who have washed their robes and made them white in the blood of the Lamb'. In ch. 11 the church is offered a paradigm of the true prophetic witness as it sets out to fulfil its vocation to prophesy before the world. Utilising the figures of Moses and Elijah that prophetic witness takes place in a social scene opposed to God where that witness must take place even though it ends up with martyrdom: 'the martyr defends not his life but his cause', as Leonardo Boff has put it.

One of the prime issues in the 'letters to the seven churches' is 'eating food sacrificed to idols', and 'immorality', almost certainly a reference to idolatry (2:14 and 2:20). The strictures against those who recommend eating food sacrificed to idols indicates the need to create some distance between the conduct of Christians and the typical behaviour of society. The references to idolatry and immorality in these passages are to be understood as in the tradition of the Jewish concern for holiness, that distinctive pattern of life over against the nations: 'it shall not be so with you. . .' (Mark

10:43). There is a challenge to the assumption that the disciple is going to be able to take part without too much comfort in the social intercourse of the contemporary world. As Klaus Wengst has recently put it.

> According to John the decisive question with which he sees the Christians of his time confronted, is not 'How can I survive this situation with the least possible harm? . . . Rather, the question of the possibility of his own survival is completely put in the shade by the one question which is important to him: In this situation, how can I bear witness to the rule of Christ, his claim to the whole world? . . . He calls for an exodus . . . as joining in, life along the usual lines, necessarily means complicity with Rome. The consequence is social separation . . . By refusing to 'join in', by contradicting and resisting, they dispute that the world belongs to those who claim to rule over it. . . . 'Here is a call for the endurance of the saints, those who keep the commandments of God and the faith of Jesus' (14:12). . . . This endurance puts Christian life into the role of the outsider. . . .[5]

Wengst reminds us of those counter-cultural strands n Revelation. Apart from the issue of meat sacrificed to idols, I can do little more at this stage than indicate other features which suggest that we have a text here which resists compromise and accommodation, and advocates keeping alive the spirit of Jesus (and the apostles in faith and practice) by an advocacy of a critical distance from contemporary culture—in the character of social relations and the language of its religious discourse. Let me offer some examples.

Firstly, the invective against complacency in the 'letters to the churches' has been interpreted as a indication of growing laxity and lack of rigour. The concern for holiness in Jewish culture was tied up with the maintenance of an alternative culture over against the nations. This can be seen in the repudiation of idolatry, the food laws, circumcision and sabbath observance. Likewise the call to martyrdom indicates the need for resistance, even if that means non-participation in the Roman economic system.

Secondly, for Revelation the spirit and prophecy have a central role as they were to have in the Montanist movement and century later. By then prophecy was viewed with suspicion, so much so that Revelation's place as part of the canon was challenged. Ambivalence with regard to prophecy has always characterised religion. Revelation stands out against those who would quench the spirit and despise prophecy. As with the messianic/millenarian/apocalyptic tradition, prophecy was too deep-rooted in the Christian memory to be allowed to be anathematised, so that other ways had to be found to domesticate it.

Finally, the apocalyptic imagery and cosmology itself betokens a view of the world where protest and resistance to compromise are the order of the day. The dualistic cosmology encouraged a separatist mentality. The millennarian horizon with its radical alternative to the present order showed up the discredited social processes of the present in the starkest possible relief. It was not just a case of relativising the world order in the light of the glory of the City of God, for it also involved casting the power behind the structures as diabolical and exposing its concerns as oppressive. There is little room for accommodation with the 'beast' and Babylon. Now all this not to suggest that the apocalyptic outlook could not be 'appropriated and neutralised' by its incorporation into the dominant ideology. Clearly that did happen to some extent, not least by its incorporation into the canon. But it was a difficult process, for such subversive ideas could never be completely tamed.

7. THE TWO POLES OF THE INTERPRETATIVE TASK

But it is inadequate to concentrate in any social hermeneutic simply on what the text meant. Of equal (if not still greater importance) is the analysis of contemporary usage, whether in academy or in Church, and the investigation of the particular interests that are being served by various patterns of interpretation. That point is neatly encapsulated in the diagram taken from the work of the Brazilian theologian, Clodovis Boff.

scripture   ourselves and our reality

↑   ↑

↓   ↓

its context   our context[7]

So the book of Revelation can be the resource of both ends of the political spectrum. On the one hand, it has been a poem of hope to oppressed Christians throughout the ages and continues to be a resource for many poor people in their struggle against injustice. On the other hand, it offers a dream of miraculous rescue at the rapture of the saints which serves as a licence for escape from political struggle. Our unease with that usage is not sufficient reason to avoid wrestling with our apocalyptic and millennarian heritage and to leave it to literalists and those bent dehumanising fanaticism. Deep down we may sympathise with Bultmann's assessment of Revelation as 'weakly Christianised Judaism', [8] a theological assessment which is as questionable as it is deeply offensive to our Jewish roots. The use made of the book of Revelation by the poor as they meet for their Bible study in the grassroots communities of the contemporary Third World church is an eloquent testimony to the fractured existence of life in a fallen world. The quest for a perfect society to which early Christianity was committed is reflected in a fragmentary way in its textual production, evidence of the constraints on the pursuit of the millennium. The eager longing for change and frustrated expectations manifest in the outbursts of vengeful anger in the songs of triumph over the fall of Babylon in Revelation are expressions of that fractured existence. Resolution is offered in the vision of hope as a necessary means of overcoming the tensions inherent in an oppressive society. The 'dangerous visions' of a messianic age offer a very different horizon of hope which seems foolishness to the prevailing culture. It is this alternative horizon to which the apocalyptic and millennarian tradition has borne witness. It has protested against those arrangements which have the appearance of order but which in reality have brought about the prosperity and progress of some at the expense of others. It is frequently those who have to bear that suffering who can see the fragility of those structures which appear to offer peace and security and find in that tradition a way of articulating their protest and a spur to their actions. Those whose lives are fragmented and who live at the margins can discern the signs of the times in ways which are frightening to those of us who cannot see from what is apparently a more favoured vantage-point. Their cries of protest and their aspirations for liberation are expressed in that longing for the manifestation of God's righteousness. It is hardly surprising that such powerful statements should be domesticated or branded as eccentric or, worse, anathematised and repressed. But they are too powerful, too deep-rooted and are a reminder of the fact that the way of the messiah can only be eclipsed and never obliterated as the Paraclete who convicts the world of sin, of righteousness and judgment never allows the work of the Messiah to die.[9]

Notes

1. From Leonardo Boff *Way of the Cross—Way of Justice* (New York 1980).
2. See Paul Ricour *Essays on Biblical Interpretation.*
3. On this see further Stuart Hall's essay 'Religious Ideologies and Social Movements in Jamaica' in R. Bocock and K. Thompson *Religion and Ideology* (Manchester 1985).
4. The interpretative approach is indebted to Frederic Jameson's *The Political Unconscious* (London 1981).
5 Klaus Wengst *Pax Romana and the Peace of Jesus Christ* (London 1987).
6. As is suggested by A. Y. Collins in her discussion of Rev. 13.15–17 in her article 'The Political Perspective of the Book of Rev.' *JBL* vol. 96.

7. From Clodovis Boff *Theology and Praxis* (English translation, New York 1987) chapter 8.

8. R. Bultmann *Theology of the New Testament* (London 1952) vol. ii p. 175.

9. See further Rowland *Radical Christianity* (Cambridge 1988) where the importance of the recovery of the millennarian and Utopian horizon in the Christian tradition is stressed. The project contrasts with the rejection of the chiliastic tradition suggested by J. Ratzinger in his essay 'Eschatology and Utopia' in *Church Ecumenism and Politics* (London 1988). His position is based on a very dubious attempt to separate both Jeremiah and Jesus from what he calls the theo-political. This does not stand up to exegetical scrutiny. Both Jesus and Jeremiah do not deny God's involvement in the process of history but reject the false views of their contemporaries as leading to destruction.

PART III

Church History: Opponents from Within and Without

Giovanni Gonnet

Cathars and Waldenses Within the Church in the Middle Ages

AROUND THE year 1000, two centres of heresy flared up almost without warning in Europe: one in Italy, at Ravenna, the other in France, in a small village in the diocese of Châlons-sur-Marne. Whereas in Ravenna the bishop condemned a certain grammarian named Vilgard for having taught 'things contrary to the faith', in Champagne a peasant by the name of Leutard, after leaving his wife *ex praecepto evangelico* in order to devote himself fully to chastity and preaching, began to smash the crucifix and other holy images and to maintain the futility of tithes. Summoned by the bishop and questioned in the presence of his followers, he was ridiculed and taken for a madman.

These two episodes show common characteristics which were to be repeated in the history of heresy in the late Middle Ages. First, they concerned simple laymen, with various levels of literacy, but without theological knowledge. What is common to them is their wish to reform something which they thought was wrong within their church, generally doing so by linking themselves directly to the Holy Scriptures. Both incur ecclesiastical censure, which proves that the Roman doctrinal authority was always ready to intervene promptly whenever attacks on orthodoxy appeared. This was not yet the actual Inquisition with its tribunals and its procedures, but, according to a practice which went back to the advice of the Apostle Paul to Titus to 'avoid heresy' (Tit. 3:10), it was the bishops' task to safeguard the faith of the believers.

The two episodes which we have just recalled were not isolated cases. In the first half of the eleventh century more or less serious instances of heresy appeared in Aquitaine, about 1017, in Orléans in 1022, in Arras in 1025, at Monforte in Piedmont in 1028, again in Champagne, and further north at Liège in Belgium and at Goslar in Germany between 1045 and 1052. The chroniclers, the regional synods, the bishops and the councils which had to look into these phenomena (out of historical curiosity or in order to fulfil the duties of their offices) put forward the idea that it was simply a matter of a revival of Manichaeism—demonstrated particularly by practices which had been observed in the past, from the sixth to the tenth century, by the ancient or recent followers of Manès, such as the Paulicians of Asia Minor or the Bogomiles of the Balkans. However that may be, the heresies thus demonstrated were called ' popular' to distinguish them from the 'theological' heresies of the preceding centuries.

After a period of 'heretical void', the twelfth century saw the rise of movements inspired by Donatism, according to the model in force at the time of the Gregorian reform taken up by the Patarenes of Milan and Florence. They are distinguished particularly by their rejection of the sacraments celebrated by priests whom they held to be unworthy, as happened in Soissons and Anvers around 1114. This form of Donatism, based on *ex opere operantis*—the Roman doctrinal authority was, on the contrary, faithful to *ex opere operato*—drove a number of believers to pursue what has humorously been described as 'liturgical boycotting'; and this is what was soon afterwards to characterise the more substantial groups of Petrobrusians, Henricians and Arnaldists. Committed to denouncing and combating them were people of high calibre such as Peter the Venerable and Bernard of Clairvaux who, shortly before Saint Dominic, travelled through the centre and south of France to ward off the danger of heresy and to revive the fortunes of the Church which had been seriously compromised by the negligence of local clergy. In this respect a letter from Saint Bernard to the Count of Toulouse has remained famous. In this letter the Abbot of Clairvaux complains that 'the churches are without congregations, the congregations without priests, and the priests without the reverence which is due to them.' All these movements—which in turn differ from the groups which preceded them or were still appearing here and there in the Rhineland, in Flanders, in Périgord, Champagne and Brittany, and whch may be generally described as 'pre-Catharist'—profess a radical evangelism which would be taken up again at the end of the twelfth and beginning of the thirteenth centuries by 'the Poor Men of Lyon' and 'the Poor Men of Lombardy', subsequently known under the common name of Waldenses. It was the time when, on the lips of the monk Henry of Cluny or the layman Vaudès of Lyon, the reply which the Apostle Peter had given to the Sanhedrin in Jerusalem rang out again: 'We ought to obey God rather than men.' (Acts 5:29) From then on, the disputing groups or movements were divided into two trends or strands: one, inspired by the oriental dualism characteristic of the Paulicians, the Bogomiles and the neo-Manichaeans would take the name of Catharism; the other, with Patarene and evangelical tendencies and centred on the basic themes of Christian ethics as they were perceived by simple folk from reading or listening to the Sermon on the Mount, would be represented particularly by Waldensianism.

Anyone wishing to group together the characteristic features of the heresies of the eleventh and twelfth centuries would first have to bring out a common basis of oppositions and negations which all emanate more or less from the necessity to reform the Church from within. This common basis is not at all heterodox in itself, but on to it would be grafted more radical tendencies which sooner or later would depart from primordial ideals. Throughout, the claim of exclusive recourse to Holy Scripture as the basic norm of faith and of the conduct of believers is dominant. That means that they resorted even then to free examination, as demonstrated by the preference given to the New Testament. On the other hand, especially with the neo-Manichaean groups, gnostic tendencies appear, such as the denial of the dogma of the Trinity, the docetist refusal to accept the Incarnation, the aversion for the cross—seen as an infamous sign of the death of Christ—the condemnation of marriage (or at least of the sexual act), and abstention from meat-eating; whereas the many rejections of the charismatic power of the Church conform more to the Donatist principles of Patarene evangelism, and are expressed in different ways, by the belittling of the sacraments, religious buildings and cemeteries, by the practice of spiritual baptism by the laying on of hands, by the ritual of the blessing of the bread which replaces the Eucharist and by the twin rejection of the intercession of the saints and the doctrine of purgatory. All these disputes have their counterbalance in the establishment of a new ecclesiology which appears especially with the Petrobrusians, the Henricians and the Waldenses. The Church—they affirm—is only a congregation of believers within which rituals are reduced to the necessary minimum, the sacraments have lost their quasi-magic character, preaching is itinerant and often performed by laymen, spiritual welfare depending exclusively on the reading of the gospels, on the reciting of the Lord's Prayer and on the mutual confession of sins. Finally, throughout this, the pauperist principle is manifest: the Church must be poor, as Christ and the Apostles were poor, hence the practice of shared wealth, the condemnation of the riches of the clergy and the refusal to pay tithes.

During the two following centuries, we witness the rise of heresy as it was manifested in its two main currents, but with this particular element: that Catharism declined gradually until it disappeared completely towards the end of the fourtheenth century, whereas Waldensianism was to survive until the present day, after allying itself at the start of the modern era with the pre-Calvinist Reformation. Catharism, preponderant especially in France and Italy, had been organised in churches, each one with its bishop. According to a Dominican of the end of the thirteenth century (Anselm of Alexandria), it was eastern in origin: some Frenchmen who were in Constantinople around 1147 after the second crusade, came into contact with some Bogomiles from Bulgaria and were converted to their ideas, founding a church on the shores of the Bosphorus; then, returning to France, they spread their new beliefs, creating churches there, in the north and south of the country, especially in Languedoc and Aquitaine, at Albi, Carcassonne, Toulouse and Agen. The Cathars of these regions, who took the name of Albigenses, professed at that time the modified dualism of the Bulgarian Bogomiles, but at a council probably held about 1167 at St Félix-de-Caraman, they adopted the absolute dualism of the Thracian Bogomiles which was already professed by a group of Italian Cathars. The latter also swayed between the two dualisms: absolute at Desenzano, modified at Concorrezzo, elements of both at Bagnolo and Vicenza, and in other towns of central Italy, in Florence, Spoleto, Orvieto and Viterbo. As for the Waldenses, after numerous condemnations by bishops, councils, the Papacy and the Inquisition, they dispersed throughout Europe from the Mediterranean to the Baltic.

Faced with such a great expansion of Catharist and Waldensian groups, the Church did not remain passive. Leaning as far as possible on the secular arm, it took up the old instruments of vigilance and repression, adjusting them to the new circumstances. In fact, although the first disputes had from the start provoked the reaction of the ecclesiastical powers in the form of the bishops (episcopal Inquisition), with Saint Bernard another method was inaugurated with public debates normally presided over by a cardinal-legate (legatine Inquisition) with the aim of convincing heretics by persuasion rather than by coercion. When this procedure failed, the Church readjusted its methods and operated on two fronts: on the one hand founding the Franciscan and Dominican Orders, on the other hand changing the bishops' process of enquiry and supervision into a genuine inquisition (monastic Inquisition). The founding of the Friars Minor and the Friars Preachers (1209 and 1216) was significant: by taking from the heretics their typically evangelical elements (the imitation of apostolic life, the genuine practice of poverty, itinerant preaching, etc.), they attempted to neutralise the charismatic credibility of the heresiarchs, turning it to their advantage. As for the monastic Inquisition, exercised by *ad hoc* tribunals whose operation was first entrusted to the Dominicans, it was formally founded at the Council of Toulouse in 1229, just at the end of the crusade against the Albigenses which had bathed the whole of the south of France in blood on the pretext of annihilating heresy once and for all.

All this naturally had a sequel: spiritual Franciscans, Béghards and Béguines, Fraticelli, Apostolics, Brethren of the Free Spirit, Wycliffites, Hussites, etc. We should look at the situation again, especially when, with the great reformers of the sixteenth century, the positions were reversed, with Rome itself being accused of heresy. . . . But that is the subject of another discourse.

Translated by Barrie Mackay

Eugène Honée

Burning heretics—a Sin against the Holy Ghost?

The Lutheran Churches and how they dealt with the Sixteenth-century Anabaptist Movement

DIFFERENCES OF belief in the sixteenth century led in Western Christendom to a multiplicity of obstinate schisms. Lutheranism, Calvinism and Anglicanism began as reform movements within Catholicism but they developed into independent confessions with their own widespread church connections in which there was no longer any place for the authority of the bishop of Rome. Alongside and over against the great churches of the Reformation there soon arose small fringe groups of Anabaptists, spiritualists and other dissenters. These dissidents were rejected and persecuted by both Catholics and Protestants: in that sense they were the stepchildren of the Reformation.

In order to characterise the relationship in which these Protestant minorities stood to the Reformation Churches that were developing R. Bainton in 1941 used an image borrowed from the modern parliamentary system: they were 'the left wing of the Reformation'. The term was intended to rehabilitate them. What the originator of it wanted to express was recognition of the fact that on all fronts, in doctrine, in spirituality and in Church order, the sixteenth century dissenters had put in the balance a greater break with tradition than their Reformation opponents. Building on Bainton's insights G. H. Williams spoke twenty years later of 'the radical Reformation'. Just like its predecessor, this label was prompted by a positive judgment.[1]

The two characterisations mentioned have in common the fact that they open up a new and favourable perspective on the reforms striven for by the dissenters. One can now ask oneself how within this perspective, once it has been chosen, the position of the majorities appears—the position of those the radicals found themselves in opposition to. Of the two Church historians mentioned it is William above all who has spoken out clearly on this point. In his view over against the radical or 'fourth' Reformation there stands the 'magisterial Reformation'. The expression, coined by Williams himself, refers on the one hand to the authority which the *magistri*, the university theologians schooled in the great doctrinal traditions, enjoyed in the three Reformation Churches, and on the other hand to the strict control which these Churches experienced and allowed on the part of the *magistratus*, the secular authorities. It is above all this latter aspect that strikes one. While the small communities of Anabaptist and other dissenters came into being through voluntary association, the Reformation Churches, just like the Catholic Church, maintained close contacts with the authorities. They developed into national or State churches.

The subject of this essay is neither the 'magisterial' nor the 'radical' Reformation but the conflict between them, the way they were at daggers drawn with each other. In particular we shall go into the fierce struggle that developed in the first half of the sixteenth century between Lutherans and Anabaptists. Not all aspects of this are on the agenda. We shall limit ourselves to clarifying two major points, the doctrinal condemnation and the persecution under the criminal law that the Anabaptists experienced from Lutherans. The first process culminated in 1530 with the publication of the first Lutheran confession of faith, the Augsburg Confession or *Confessio Augustana*. The second was carried out by means of a great series of penal measures taken by Lutheran princes and town councils against Anabaptist groups before and after the Augsburg Confession was issued.

It would be wrong to suppose that in the first case, that of the Augsburg Confession, we are dealing with an ecclesiastical initiative or that on the other hand it was the secular authorities alone that were responsible for the persecutions. The first Lutheran confession of faith was signed by those who wielded secular power, in other words by some princes and representatives of town councils. There were those who at the imperial diet of Augsburg, after which the confession is named, gave an account of their faith and, we must immediately add, of the faith of the Evangelical congregations they had taken under their protection, and did so before the Emperor and the remaining estates of the empire. In other words, the ecclesial communities were indeed present in the Augsburg Confession as those responsible for their confession of faith, but indirectly through the agency of those who wielded Christian power and authority.

Similarly the penal measures enacted against the Anabaptists before and after their doctrinal condemnation were not the work of the secular authorities alone. Through their clergy and theologians the churches were involved in drawing them up. Melanchthon, Luther, Johannes Brenz and others provided the theoretical justification for the penalties incurred by the Anabaptists. Their advice could differ considerably, and thus also the measures that they helped prepare. In other words, just as with the doctrinal condemnation, what we have here is the combined effect of a number of powers and responsibilities.

1. THE REPUDIATION OF ANABAPTIST DOCTRINE

No complete, rounded picture of Anabaptist doctrine is given in the Augsburg Confession (AC). Here and there, often incidentally, it enumerates a number of Anabaptist doctrinal positions to be repudiated. At first sight the selection seems arbitrary, and it is hardly possible to indicate an Anabaptist group which would have been identified with all or most of the condemned positions. Some scholars, especially those with a Menonite background or outlook, go so far as to assert that the different judgments taken together evoke a completely distorted picture of the Anabaptist movement. But this reproach cannot be justified. Anyone who realises that the person who drafted the Augsburg Confession, Mclanchthon, was from his own experience acquainted especially with the Anabaptism that was propagated in central Germany from 1526 onwards can with a little trouble recognise certain features of this particular type in the often very generally expressed judgments that are made about Anabaptists in general. What is involved is a form of Anabaptism that is *sui generis* and that from many points of view is distinct from the Anabaptist movement that at the same time was being spread from Switzerland into southern Germany. While the Swiss form of Anabaptism had an explicitly humanist and biblicist streak, central German Anabaptism nourished itself strongly from the traditions of a popular form of German mysticism. Just as these traditions had been manifested earlier in Thomas Müntzer, the 'mystic with the hammer' who lost his life in the Peasants' Revolt, so they turned up again shortly after the end of this rebellion (1525) in figures like Hans Hut, Melchior Rink and other Anabaptist leaders.[2]

In the Augsburg Confession a number of controversies with Anabaptism are broached, but we can properly limit our consideration to three major points: the difference of views of justification, on baptism, and on social morality.[3] The first of these questions is raised in article 5 which concludes with a condemnation of 'the Anabaptists and others who teach that we can receive the Holy Spirit without the outward word of the Gospel, through our own preparations and works'. What do these enigmatic words mean? The context is none other than the exposition of the doctrine of justification, which begins in AC 4 and continues until AC 6. It is through faith alone that justification and forgiveness of sins are obtained, article 4 teaches. And according to AC 6 faith once acquired brings forth good fruit of itself. The question in the intervening article 5 is the order whereby this sanctifying faith is obtained. The Lutherans emphasise here that the Spirit awakens it in us by means of two external means of grace entrusted to the Church's ministry, the word proclaimed and the sacraments ministered. In the repudiation quoted above the Anabaptists were clearly reproached with neglecting these objective means of grace. Just like Thomas Müntzer, they were regarded as spiritualists for whom what matters is the inner self-revelation of the Spirit which is prepared for by spiritual exercises.

The description given in AC 5 of Anabaptist spirituality is correct but also concise. It does not let it emerge that for the opponent the issue is the interiorisation of belief. Rink contrasted the dead faith taught by the Lutherans with the living and personally experienced faith Müntzer had spoken of. For him just as for Müntzer the process of believing was something quite conscious and also painful, in the course of which a person lost his or her links with this world and was re-born to become a new creature. In this vision justification is at the same time also a process of sanctification: man is changed and becomes capable of fulfilling God's commandments.

In the theological train of thought of AC 5 to 7 the emphasis is put quite strongly on God's transcendence and on the objective means of grace whereby salvation is offered. The position that is condemned is marked by contrasting features: here it is a question of God's immanence, of the internal experience of faith and the practice of the Christian life. This opposition is continued in the controversy over baptism, which is broached in AC 9.

For the Anabaptists baptism is the symbol of the conversion described above and of inner rebirth. Baptism should be withheld from all who have not yet been through a process of conversion or have not yet developed an awareness of faith (newborn children). The scriptural justification for this ruling was taken from Mark 16:16: 'He who believes and is baptised will be saved'. The sequence described here could not be deviated from. Faith must unconditionally precede baptism. In this vision the act of baptism does not bestow divine grace but is a sign made by the person receiving baptism himself or herself. It sets the seal on his or her faith, is his or her solemn pledge to follow Christ in a holy amendment of life. Apart from a covenant with Christ baptism also sets the seal on a covenant with one's brothers and sisters, with the others who have been chosen for holiness.

For Lutherans this radical re-interpretation of baptism was an abomination. According to a preliminary study for AC 9, the 'signs and works of God' had been downgraded by the Anabaptists to become 'signs and words among Christians'. The final text pronounces a solemn anathema over the rejection of infant baptism and emphasises that baptism is a sacrament in which 'grace is offered' to men and women from outside. The connection between sacramental sign and faith is not mentioned in AC 9. From contemporary commentaries we can deduce that Luther and the Wittenberg theologians counted faith among the gifts bestowed in baptism. They found it clearly inadmissible to put faith and awareness on the same footing without more ado. The process of understanding the salvation offered in baptism belonged, according to them alone essentially to the *growth* of faith, not to faith itself.[4]

The third and final difference concerns the social and ethical implications of the faith on which baptism sets the seal. The radical renewal of existence must according to the Anabaptists manifest itself too in Christians' social behaviour. Being formed in the likeness of Christ obliged them to follow literally the prescriptions of the Sermon on the Mount. They do not sit as magistrates or on town councils because every exercise of authority involves the use of power or violence. They do not take any oaths and refuse military service. One would expect the Lutherans to have stigmatised these views of the Anabaptists primarily as a new form of legalism, in other words as a renewed attempt to obtain justification through works. But the Augsburg Confession deals with these teachings in article 16, which covers secular authority and the attitude which Christians should adopt towards the State. In other words, they were regarded as undermining and authority of governments.

The particular perspective in which the Anabaptists' social ethics cropped up evokes the question how those concerned judged the secular authority that had been placed over them. Broadly speaking two views were current within the Anabaptism of central Germany. Most groups consisted of 'silent Anabaptists' who did indeed adopt a distanced attitude with regard to the authorities but were at least intent on subverting the existing order. They did not maintain that one was obliged to offer the princes or town magistrates no obedience but took the line that precisely because these latter possessed secular power and appreciated it they were not Christians. The followers of Hans Hut however went a stage further. They too preached non-violence, but this was linked to a limitation of time. With Thomas Müntzer they judged that the rulers had in principle forfeited the right to wield the sword.

They had not used this right in order to renew society radically in keeping with God's word. Their dominion should therefore soon be broken. Hut predicted that the Lord's second coming would soon take place and portrayed this as a bloody final judgment that would be carried out on the princes. The alliance of true Christians lived in the tense expectation of this final judgment and at the same time saw itself as the instrument with which God would execute his punishment.[5]

In the Augsburg Confession this apocalyptic Anabaptism is explicitly mentioned and condemned, but in the context of article 17 which deals with the Lord's second coming. This version does not come up for discussion in AC 16 which we are dealing with here, just as the opposing view of the 'silent' Anabaptists is also indeed passed over in silence. In this article what is being got at is an opinion shared by both silent and revolutionary Anabaptists that 'it is not lawful for Christians to occupy secular offices'. The opposing point of view is defended with a reference to the divine origin of secular authority. Because the authority of government is created and established by God a Christian can without sinning be a prince, magistrate or judge, punish with the sword, and conduct just wars.

2. THE PERSECUTION OF THE ANABAPTISTS

It is striking that in the three articles of the Augsburg Confession discussed above an anathema is repeated pronounced against Anabaptists. 'The Churches among us condemn [*damnant*] the Anabaptists', the signatories of the confession declare as often as three times. All the more weight should be accorded to this anathema because the Anabaptists were the only opponents against whom it was used. Not just the Roman Catholics but even the Zwinglians, detested because of their deviant eucharistic doctrine, were spared this formula of condemnation in the Augsburg Confession. The debate with these groups of dissentients was conducted in quite a different and indeed ecumenical style. While one distanced oneself from their views, this was always done in cautious terms and without explicitly naming them. The Anabaptists on the other hand were identified as a group and then branded as heretics. With regard to them one did not feel oneself bound to demonstrate any respect, brotherly love or exumenical openness.

The harsh judgment pronounced by the Augsburg Confession on the Anabaptists is to a certain extent understandable if we consider that the princes and town councillors who signed this confession in 1530 had co-operated a year earlier in passing an imperial law that outlawed the

Anabaptists. At the imperial diet of Speyer in 1529 a decree was issued against the Anabaptists in which re-baptism was characterised as a serious offence which deserved to be punished by death. The decree was issued in the name of the Emperor but was greeted with equal agreement by the Catholic and Lutheran estates. It was thus included among the imperial diet's legibly valid decisions.[6] The Augsburg Confession's anathema follows unquestionably from the imperial law issued a year earlier. Both items had as their basis the same fundamental insight, that Anabaptist were heretics.

In the 1529 decree the description of re-baptism as an offence and the choice of punishment were justified by a reference to the old imperial law, the Code of Justinian. At first sight this historical foundation may surprise, but it was not at all something plucked out of thin air. The Code we have mentioned did in fact incorporate a number of laws which predecessors of Justinian in the fourth century had issued against the practice of re-baptism. This legislation was directed against the early Christian sect of the Donatists, who practised re-baptism on a large scale and administered it to all Christians who wanted to join their community. In their fight against Donatism the Christian emperors of the fourth century stigmatised re-baptism as sacrilege and therefore demanded the death penalty in their laws. The 1529 referred back to this legislation. In other words Charles V and the German estates of the realm reactivated the old imperial law that still remained in force. In common decision they took at Speyer the Anabaptists of their own time were in fact identified with a group of notorious heretics from the past, the Donatists. In that way one could deal with them most effectively. Anyone who went in for re-baptism or let himself or herself be re-baptised was clearly a heretic and was therefore punished with death.

Co-operating in passing a law and putting it into effect are two different actions. The Lutheran princes and municipalities did not simply model their proceedings against the Anabaptists on the 1529 decree. Claus Peter Clasen has worked out that in the period from 1525 to 1618 about eight hundred and forty-five Anabaptists were executed in Europe, and that of these executions eighty-four per cent took place in regions that had remained Catholic, especially the Hapsburg terroritoires and Bavaria, while only sixteen per cent were carried out in areas under Protestant rule. The vast majority of the latter percentage is accounted for by the Reformed canton of Berne. Obviously the Lutheran authorities had relatively few Anabaptists executed. It is even definitely established that a large proportion of Lutheran jurisdiction—Hess, the Palatinate, Wüttemberg, and a number of imperial cities—never applied the death penalty to Anabaptists. That means at the very least that they were prepared to grant them religious freedom. The

Anabaptists were just as much persecuted by these rulers, but the highest penalties they exacted against them were banishment and lengthy terms of imprisonment. As a matter of fact only one Protestant territory in Germany can be indicated where the imperial decree was strictly observed: the Lutheran electorate of Saxony, where according to Clasen twenty-one executions were carried out—that is, a quarter of the total that can be attributed to Protestant rules.[7] Two questions arise from these figures. How did it come about that the Lutheran rules in general applied milder punishments than their Catholic and even Reformed counterparts? And how on the other hand can we explain the fact that of all places it should be Saxony, the birthplace of Lutheranism, than deviated from the policy maintained elsewhere?

Undoubtedly the course of action that is characteristic for the majority of Protestant states is bound up with the very strong spread and influence of Luther's doctrine of the two kingdoms. This doctrine offered Protestant rules and their advisers a different view of the phenomenon of heresy and one that departed from the Catholic tradition. Already during the quarrel over indulgences Luther launched an attack on the traditional law that had been developed during the Middle Ages with regard to heretics and heresy. 'To burn heretics is against the will of the Holy Spirit', he had asserted in 1518 in an elucidation of his famous theses on indulgences.[8] And two years later in his *Letter to the Christian nobility of Germany* of 1520 we find: 'Heretics must be conquered by writings, not by fire. If the trick were to conquer heretics with fire then executioners would be the most learned scholars of the entire world'.[9] Against the background of these statements stands the sharp distinction that Luther wished to see drawn between the Gospel and the world, between the spiritual and the worldly kingdom. For him heresy was like a wrong but obstinately maintained conviction of belief which could only be overcome in a spiritual and religious way, in other words by the preaching of God's word. Here there is no job for secular government because it has no power over people's inner thoughts and beliefs. When it claims to prescribe a particular religious conviction it oversteps its competence and destroys the order willed by God. In his much-read treatise of 1523 *On secular government and the extent to which one must obey it* Luther repeats his basic insight and at the same time gives it his most classical formulation: 'Given that everyone must decide in his conscience how he believes or does not believe and that thereby no damage is done to secular authority, this authority must be content with restricting itself to its own tasks and let everyone believe as he can or will and not constrain anyone by force'.[10]

Luther's words have an extraordinarily modern ring to them as a plea for religious freedom in the fullest sense of the term. But they did not have that effect, nor could they, in sixteenth-century society. Nor was that their intention. Luther and most of his contemporaries found it something taken for granted that government should tolerate only one doctrine within its jurisdiction. In their eyes any other solution would necessarily lead to civil dissension. Hence the Anabaptists were later kept down and silence was forced on them through banishment or imprisonment. At the same time the Reformer's statements on matters of principle brought many contemporaries to the view that one should not deprive dissenters of their life for talking of their religious convictions. All that was allowed was stopping the free propagation of their views. In other words Luther's view did indeed have a pioneering significance for the theory and practice of law of his age. We can deduce this influence from the way Protestant states dealt with the imperial law of 1529: most of them did not give a damn. And when two years after it had been promulgated it was once again on the agenda of a conference of Protestant states most of those present declared that they did not regard themselves as in any way bound by it. Their point of view was that it went back to an imperial decision that was proclaimed without proper discussion and precipitately.

Finally just a word about the strict administration of the law in the electorate of Saxony. It was dictated by the political conviction that the Anabaptists were not dissenters but rebels. The Elector and his council regarded Anabaptism as a consequence of the Peasants' Revolt of a few years before, as a fire still smouldering from the revolutionary movement unleashed by Thomas Müntzer. The Wittenberg theologians, especially Luther and Melanchthon, shared these politicians' view and confirmed them in it. In fact, even Luther came to regard Anabaptism more and more as a movement of rebellion which as such fell under the competence to punish of secular government. When heresy was coupled with revolution it no longer fell under the law of love which rules in the spiritual kingdom but under the avenging justice that is exercised in the secular kingdom. Leaders and obdurate followers of a rebellious sect therefore deserved the death penalty.[11]

In principle everyone in the Lutheran camp, governments as well as theologians, could subscribe to this line of argument which operated completely within the paradigm of the two kingdoms. It was the question of fact, the question whether the Anabaptists one had to deal with really came under suspicion of revolution, that aroused the difference of opinion. Again and again when this question came up Johannes Brenz, the minister of Schwäbisch Hall and adviser to various princes and city magistrates, was much more cautious in his judgments than his Wittenberg Colleagues.[12]

The latter however were actually confronted in their region by disturbances caused by Anabaptists. Luther and Melanchthon were indeed right when they ascribed revolutionary aims to some Anabaptists. We have already seen that Hans Hut's followers avowed a chiliastic form of Anabaptism. One can perhaps reproach the Wittenberg theologians with having lumped all Anabaptists together and having ascribed to all of them one and the same doctrine destined to stir up revolt. They certainly were aware of the distinction between 'silent' and apocalyptic Anabaptists but did not take it seriously. The devil, Melanchthon observed on one occasion, disguised himself in various shapes but could not hide his cloven hoof.[13] What this meant was that all Anabaptists were possessed by the same spirit of revolt that had fatally manifested itself in Thomas Müntzer.

Translated by Robert Nowell

Notes

1. R. Bainton 'The Left Wing of the Reformation' in *The Journal of Religion* 21 (1941) pp. 124–151; G. H. Williams *The Radical Reformation* (Philadelphia 1962).

2. For a full description of the Anabaptist movement in central Germany see J. S. Oyer *Lutheran Reformers against Anabaptists* (The Hague 1964) pp. 41–113.

3. For the text of the Augsburg Confession see *Die Bekenntnis schriften der evangelisch-lutherischen Kirche* (Göttingen 1973) pp. 31–137.

4. K. H. zur Mühlen 'Luthers Tauflehre und seine Stellung zu den Täufern' in H. Junghans (ed.) *Leben und Werk Martin Luthers von 1526 bis 1546* two volumes (Göttingen 1983) vol. I pp. 119–138, vol. II pp. 765–770.

5. G. Seebass art. 'Hans Hut' in *Theologische Realenzyklopädie* vol. 15 (1986) cols. 741–747.

6. For the text of this decree see *Deutsche Reichstagsakten unter Kaiser Karl V* vol. 7/2 (Stuttgart 1935) pp. 1325ff. A balanced interpretation is offered by H. J. Goertz *Die Täufer. Geschichte und Deutung* (Munich 1980) pp. 127ff.

7. C. P. Clasen *Anabaptism: a social history* (Ithaca/London 1972) pp. 358ff.

8. Martin Luther *Werke. Kritische Gesamtausgabe* (Weimar 1883 onwards) (WA) vol. I p. 624.

9. WA vol. VI p. 455

10. WA vol. XI p. 264

11. For a detailed treatment of the subject of Luther and the Anabaptists see the fundamental article by W.Köhler art. 'Martin Luther' in *Mennonitisches Lexikon* 2 (1937) pp. 702–708 and Gottfried Seebass 'Luthers Stellung zur Verfolgung der Täufer und ihre Bedeutung für den deutschen Protestantismus' in *Mennonitische Geschichtsblätter* 40 (NF 35) 1983 pp. 7–24.

12. There are three memoranda on the persecution of Anabaptists: see Johannes Brenz *Werke. Eine Studienausgabe* edited by M. Brecht and G. Schäfer Früschriften

Teil 2 (Tübingen 1974) pp. 472–540. For the interpretation of these texts see Gottfried Seebass 'An sint persequendi haeretici? Die Stellung des Johannes Brenz zur Verfolgung der Täufer', in *Blätter für Württembergische Kirchengeschichte* 70 (1970) pp. 40° 99.

13. See R. Stupperich *Melanchthons Werke in Auswalh* vol. I (Gütersloh 1951) p. 304.

Marjorie Reeves

Opponents of Antichrist: A Medieval Perception

IN MEDIEVAL tradition Antichrist[1] could be multiple, the cosmic embodiment of evil perpetually threatening the Church, or focused in a single figure to appear in end-time. In the latter form there soon developed a complete life history which was widely disseminated through Adso's tenth-century *Libellus de Antichristo*.[2] The essence of this legend was that in every respect—birth, career, preaching, miracles—Antichrist must be the sinister mirror image of Christ to deceive the faithful. The horror of Antichrist lies primarily in his ability to lead the faithful into the worship of the false god until the terrible day when the scales fall from their eyes and they know themselves to be lost. Thus the role of those who oppose Antichrist is the seemingly impossible one of proclaiming that which so plausibly masquerades as truth to be falsehood. Christ had warned against false prophets, but Antichrist and his minions will be so convincing: above all faithful watchers feared the lie dressed as truth.

Against the lie of Antichrist there was only one weapon: witness to the truth. Witness is vulnerable and lonely, exposing itself to opposition and eventually violence from without and to doubts within. The symbol for the faithful witness was given to medieval Christians in the figures of the two witnesses in the Apocalypse who prophecy against the manifested Antichrist (Rev. 11:7, 8). Their isolation is emphasised, for the peoples refuse them burial and they lie exposed until after three and a half days God resurrects them and great fear falls on all. The ministry and martyrdom of the two witnesses becomes an essential episode in the medieval scenario of 'Last Things': they occupy a large place in commentaries and form a common theme in literature and illustrations. At an early stage this role is linked with the expectation of the returning Elijah who is named as the champion against Antichrist by Justin Martyr, Commodian, Victorinus and others. The second witness was soon identified as Enoch, by Tertullian and Irenaeus, for instance. Both were seen as Old Testament types of Christ and therefore when they challenge the mighty edifice of falsehood erected by Antichrist he raves against them as representative of his supreme enemy.

In the late twelfth century Joachim and Fiore, one of the most original of Biblical exegetes, gave a radically new twist to the interpretation of these figures which had important consequences. He seems to have been aware that he was breaking with tradition for through several pages of exposition he discusses the views of the Fathers on these unnamed witnesses of the Apocalypse.[3] Literally they may be Elijah and Enoch (or more probably Moses), but spiritually—according to the *intellectus typicus*—they are two new orders of clerics and monks. There is no space here to outline Joachim's theology of history. The key point is that he departed from the Augustinian interpretation of history by affirming that a third stage (*status*) of history remained yet to come after the destruction of Antichrist in which the full work of the Spirit would be accomplished before the Second Advent. The crucial role of witnessing during the final tribulation and of leading the Church into the peace and illumination of the third *status* was to be played by two new orders of spiritual men. Joachim found these prefigured in many 'twos' of the old and New Testaments—such as the raven and dove of Noah and, of course, the two witnesses—and constantly in his writings announced their near advent.[4]

This powerful vision of contemporary men called by God in *novissimis diebus* to a special role against Antichrist attracted many but most distinctively the rigorist group in the Franciscan Order. In the mid-thirteenth century there was a strong sense of the impending 'End': the world was moving swiftly to its final crisis and this called urgently for champions to sustain the faithful against Antichrist and to convert Jews and pagans. This eschatological sense of mission emerges in a joint encyclical issued in 1255 by the Franciscan and Dominican Generals: symbolised in a series of Biblical 'twos', including the two witnesses, their orders are called in this latest age to save the world.[5] Ubertino da Casale, one of the Franciscan *zelanti*, saw Francis and Dominic typified in the returning Elijah and Enoch,[6] while Franciscans who carried their preaching to far places were motivated by the drive to fulfil the role of the witnesses.

In the late thirteenth and fourteenth centuries a further turn was given to the interpretation of the 'Last Age' by Franciscan zealots who fought ardently to keep the Rule and Testament of Francis in every detail against those who sought a common-sense relaxation of the absolute poverty enjoined by their founder. Influenced by Joachim's vision of the third *status*, the zealots began to identify their ideal of absolute poverty with the future Age of the Spirit. The onslaught of Antichrist must first be met and as witnesses to the truth they guarded the faithful must suffer, but the key to the *ecclesia spiritualis* of the future lay in their hands. It was only a short step from this position to the indentification of Antichrist with those who denied this vision and persecuted the zealots for clinging to it. The question of authority was raised in an acute form when the zealots juxtaposed the 'carnal Church' to the 'spiritual Church' of their ideal. Joachim himself, while never wavering in loyalty to the latin church, had identified one of the Antichrist manifestations in the Apocalypse with a pseudo-pope who would sit in the seat of Peter. Under sharp persecution both by the Franciscan Order and the Inquisition, extremists among the zealots began to identify the Roman Church with the 'Babylonish Whore' and the 'Pope as Antichrist'. An acute case of the tension between authority and witness to passionately held truth is seen in the writings of the Franciscan scholastic, Petrus Johannis Olivi, who greatly feared the powers of Antichrist in high places yet never literally equated the 'carnal Church' with Rome.[7]

Who were the saints and who were the antichrists? This question haunted the troubled church history of the fourteenth century. Complex characters such as Ubertino da Casale and Angelo da Clareno (leaders of the zealots) found the tension almost intolerable.[8] But for some simpler souls the answer was plain: Pope John XXII, persecutor of the champions of absolute poverty, was the Antichrist, or one of them. In the conflict the zealots were eliminated from the Order and excommunicated by the Church. Driven out and marginalised, they gathered into wandering groups of Fraticelli and so-called Beguins, developing the mentality of the 'saving remnant'. A Fraticelli letter declares that 'gathered in the ark of the true Church, they must endure and ride out the storm, for *senpre gli molti hanno gli pochi fideli de Cristo perseguitati*'.[9] In the south of France and parts of Spain the role of the intellectual Olivi passed to a humbler group of Franciscan tertiaries and other lay folk who treasured Olivi's writings in the vernacular and looked for the triumph of the *ecclesia spiritualis* after the sharp persecution of the Antichrist. Their testimony is movingly set down in the records of the Inquisition at Toulouse.[10] In Catalonia a similar group has been brought to light in a mid-fourteenth century work, the *Breviloquium*, which is an updated version of Joachim's vision of the future.[11] The faithful remnant must expect the worst before the eventual triumph of their 'truth'. So the little flock to whom the work is addressed is urged to be vigilant, to watch and pray, for they guard the treasure of the future.

Radical groups who in the later Middle Ages thus cast themselves in the role of witnesses to a final 'truth' against what they conceived to be the Antichrist in high places form an important element in the protest against an increasingly powerful ecclesiastical hierarchy. They do not of course, contain the whole story of 'the saints' in conflict with Antichrist, but I have selected this theme because it highlights the age-long problem of authority in conflict with beliefs fanatically held as truths to be defended against antichrists in whatever guise they appear.

Notes

1. For a detailed study of the medieval Antichrist legend, see R. K. Emmerson *Antichrist in the Middle Ages* (Manchester 1981).

2. *Ibid.* pp. 76–7, on Adso's *Libellus*.

3. Joachim of Fiore *Expositio in Apocalypsim* (Venice 1527, reprinted Frankfurt a. Main 1964), ff. 146–149v.

4. See references in M. Reeves *The Influence of Prophecy in the Later Middle Ages* (Oxford 1969), pp. 142–3.

5. Quoted *ibid.* p. 146.

6. Ubertino da Casale *Arbor vite crucifixe* (Venice 1485), ff. 229r–230r.

7. Reeves, *op.cit.* pp. 407–8.

8. *Ibid.* pp. 211–12, 408–10.

9. L. Oliger 'Documenta inedita ad historiam Fraticellorum spectantium', *Archivum Franciscanorum Historicum* iv (1911), p. 697.

10. See P.a Limborch *Historia Inquisitionis cui subjungitur Liber Sententiarum Inquisitionis Tholosanae 1307–1323* (Amsterdam 1692).

11. This will shortly be published by the Pontifical Institute, Toronto.

Anton Weiler

Christianity and the Rest: The Medieval Theory of a Holy and Just War

1. INTRODUCTION

ONE OF the fundamental beliefs of the Catholic Church, and one which it has included in its creed, is that its faith is 'catholic': that is, all-embracing. No one is excluded from the Catholic community of faith because of some elementary difference. In principle, the Catholic faith does not acknowledge that there is anyone outside it. All men and women are summoned to a single faith, and all are children of one and the same Father.

In reality, however, though the Catholic community has had and has many communicant members, many more people—from conviction moreover—do not (wish to) belong to that communion. What, then, throughout history, has been the Catholic attitude to such outsiders?

In his historico-theological *The City of God*, Augustine (354–430) adumbrated the doctrine of the two cities. The human world is divided into two communities: the city of God, which consists of those who wish to live in accordance with the Spirit, and the earthly city, which comprises those who wish to live in accordance with the flesh.[1] But these two communities are intermixed. The good and the bad will live alongside one another without distinction until the end of this world. What is more, in the Augustinian view, the city of worldly people is not identical with the secular State, and the city of God is not the same as the Church. God alone knows whom he has chosen ultimately, and who finally is lost.

But how were the relations to one another of the two communities conceived, when Church and State were comprised in a medieval Christendom, and together seemed already to form the city of God on earth, as Bishop Otto von Freising declared in his *History of the Two States* (1146)?[2] What is the relation of Christians on the one hand to outsiders on the other hand? Are the 'wicked' outside and are they entitled to go on living when they persecute Christians? And what is the relation to the 'wicked' in their own sphere, to the heretics and schismatics who do not wish to range themselves on the side of the central notion of one truth, one Church, and one kingdom? May Christians use force in order to ensure that the truth of one faith prevails? Are they entitled to extirpate heretics and unbelievers if they refuse to be converted?

These questions apply to the period when the Church-cum-State community's conception of itself as the one medieval Christendom developed (the last quarter of the eleventh century)[3] It is also apposite to ask how theologians and jurists in the Middle Ages tried religiously, morally and legally to justify the existence of war between Christians and pagans, and even between Christians. It is also interesting to see which rules and definitive criteria they evolved in order to make the public use of force against the enemy accord with Christian principles.

2. THE ORIGINS OF THE DOCTRINE OF THE JUST WAR

From the time of Constantine (c. 280–337), a general authority prevailed which was able to guarantee peace, security and the maintenance of public order, in a Christian commonwealth. The evangelical injunction, 'Love your enemies and pray for those who persecute you' (Matt 5:44; Lk 6:27 and 35) could not constitute the rule of general conduct for public authority, when the national community as a whole was attacked and its continued existence was threatened. Was it then permissible for Christian to repel force with force, or was it necessary for a Christian, even in the case of public hostilities between states, to obey the injunction: 'To him who strikes you on the cheek, offer the other also' (Luke 6:29)? The evangelical counsel of love for one's fellow human being to the extent even of love for one's enemies, would seem to demand that Christians should always practise non-violence in human conflicts. But does that mean that all other human values, such as self-preservation, holding on to one's own property, and standing up for the weak and defenceless, are subordinate to non-violence? If, say, an enemy threatens individual and collective security, what is a Christian people or a Christian ruler to do about this public enemy? Is the evangelical counsel something which also has to be followed in mutual relations between states?

When considering such problems, medieval pundits drew on texts from Graeco-Roman antiquity and from Judaeo-Christian tradition. They combined elements from both worlds, from the profane and from the 'sacred' societies which they knew from history, and formed a new code of conduct, the doctrine of the just war.

They took from the Romans the legal assessment of the concept of war. According to the Romans, mutual relations between states were comparable to those between individuals. In the case of a transgression of the law, the injured state was entitled to compensation in order to redress the damage and, if needs be, take it from the citizens of the other state—ultimately by the use of force in war. War was always acceptable in order to repel an enemy or for the purposes of retaliation, for the defence of allies, and in order to take back stolen goods, provided that the use of violence was announced beforehand. The Romans were able to make this legal arrangement of a conflict situation harmonise with the stoical and aristocratic way of life, which demanded moderation in action and due attention to the proportions of the conflict. In a just war, however, the imprisonment of citizens, the laying waste of the enemy's land and the sacking of cities were permissible. There was the right to wage war (*ius ad bellum*) and legal relations within it (*ius in bello*). Cicero (106–43 BC) offered the most emphatic expression of this doctrine.[4]

The Greeks, in the person of Aristotle, recognised war as a means of initiating their civilising task in regard to the barbarian nations, and as a means of self-defence.[5]

Medieval theoreticians were acquainted with the Old Testement idea of the chosen people of God fighting against their enemies. The holy war was always part of the heritage of Israel as a nation: enemies were annihilated at God's command and their land impounded. The narratives of the appearances of Joshua, of Gideon, and of the Maccabees speak of war as desired and directed by God.[6] The justification of violence was secured in the fact that war was conceived as something undertaken *at God's command.*

The New Testament instead clearly puts forward a pacifist message. The sword should remain in the scabbard; revenge is something to be left to God; and evil should not be resisted.[7] The duty of a ruler to maintain order and to punish wrongdoing is recognised,[8] but Christians are to aim at a relationship of spiritual meekness in respect of an enemy, and the letting of blood is rejected.

In the reign of Constantine, Christians had to fulfil their civic duty and could not stand aside in anti-social pacifism. They had the moral duty to obey the ruler, and to do so too when he ordered a war to defend the empire against the barbarians or even against heretics. Bishop Ambrose of Milan (c. 339–397) fused the Roman and Judaeo-Christian elements. In accordance with Ciceronian principles, the emperor could conduct a just war, but the Church was charged with the cure of souls. The correct pious disposition would keep a Christian pure in God's eyes while he was fulfilling his duty.[9]

St Augustine (354–430) went even further in the fusion of Romano-legal and Judaeo-Christian thought. For him war was a permissible means of the re-establishment of peace and of injured justice, and of punishing wrongdoers. When this moral intention is the mainspring and the intention is pure (*recta intentio*), the waging of war in order to correct injustice is justifiable: 'For it is the injustice of the opposing side that lays on the wise man the duty of waging [just] wars'.[10] The moral responsibility for the war is borne by public authority. The Christian soldier must obey as long as the government does not expressly offend against God's law.

In this view, the Ciceronian norm is subsequently extended. It is not merely the recovery of stolen goods and the restoration of injured injustice which justify a war, but—in Augustine's view—the maintenance and protection of the moral order and the punishment of evildoers comprise an acceptable war aim. It is morally justifiable to put down heretics and to overcome pagan peoples by means of force, provided that the intention is pure. *In this view, the Old Testament situation effectively exists within the Christian empire.* The enemies of God are the enemies of the empire. Christians have the duty of defending God's kingdom and of enabling it to prevail. Clearly there was a considerable change in reasoning here as the enemies of the realm were transformed into enemies of God. The identification of the State with the moral good and the marking of outsiders as enemies of God, together with a far-going denial of existing law, produced a disputable moral justification of war which was intended to identify imperial interests with God's interests. The Christian State taught people to think in Old Testament categories. The new people of God made it their task to take up weapons against evildoers.

3. CRUSADES AND INQUISITION

This was the perspective of Charlemagne (742–814), known as defender of the Church. The pope asked for military aid against the Saracens. The forceful conversion of heretics was still rejected at first, as was the participation of priests in war. But a *bellum Christi*, a 'war of Christ'— waged on papal initiative against the Church's enemies—was soon adjudged acceptable and possible. In 1095 Pope Urban II preached a crusade at the Council of Clermont.[11] The Holy War made its effective entry into the Christian world. Christendom, ruled by pope and emperor, identified itself with the kingdom of God, and maintained its own existence and rights in the name of God with the sword—and extirpated the unbelievers. Only the one truth and the one liturgy had a right to be maintained and the fight was fought to that end with full commitment. 'It is God's will' was the crusaders' cry, and the unbelievers were slaughtered in his Name.[12]

The inquisition[13] began to reflect the harsh regime of the one truth. Deviant individuals were not tolerated within Christendom and the government wielded the sword within and without under the Church's governance. Priestly power dominated the community *ad intra* and *ad extra*. Moral judgments were transformed into violent action for the sake of the Kingdom of God.

Crusades and funeral pyres were the ferocious means of maintaining one's own theocratic identity by recourse to the evangelical message of Jesus Christ. The figure of St Francis of Assisi simultaneously represented the evangelical inspiration of non-violent preaching of the message of divine love to all people.

4. JURISTS AND CANONISTS ON THE JUST WAR

The medieval practitioners of secular law.[14] adopted the Roman doctrine concerning the justification of war, and upheld the principles of self-defence, of proportional counter-measures, of the observance of the *ius gentium* and of the duty of trying first to settle the dispute by peaceful means and before some tribunal before committing an act of war.

It was the division of the early medieval empire into national kingdoms, and then into feudal sovereign states, dukedoms and earldoms, which in their turn were divided into large manors and seignorities, that often tried to obtain autonomy by the use of force; this destroyed the cohesion of the principle of justice. Every big or small monarch or prince could apply the Roman legal rules for himself, and thus conceive of a defensive war as a lawful war, as long as it remained within the bounds set.

In the realm of ecclesiastical law, after the composition c. 1140 of Gratian's *Decretum* or concordance of canon law, the emphasis in the line of tradition was placed on appropriate spiritual status and on the duty of obeying the orders of the legal ruler.[15] Concern about the right moral context of a disposition in the pursuit of war dominated among the canon lawyers. Henry of Segusia (Hostiensis c. 1270), for example, declared that it was always just for believers to undertake a war against unbelievers on the authority of the pope as the ruler of Christendom, and to wage a war on the authority of (ecclesiastical) justice in order to maintain order. Private wars waged by lesser seigneurs were, he thought, *always unjust* as was the use of warlike force in order to resist a just war.[16] Laurentius Hispanus (c. 1210) was concerned with the correct religious construction which strives for the establishment of justice and not for the allocation of punishment.[17]

One is constantly made aware of the ambiguity of thought about war. On the one hand, the use of force was accepted with certain definite legal stipulations: on the other hand, emphasis was placed on the purity of motives and the duty of obedience. There are moral considerations which can justify war. The nature of the reasons for war remain central: the defence and elevation of the good, the suppression of the bad, the establishment of universal peace and the restoration of injured rights, were recognised by the canonists as major moral values which justify violent action. This moral theological understanding of the occasion of war, of *justa causa*, extends the possibilities of war much further than the Roman legal rules allowed. An elevated moral intention is sufficient justification for war, certainly when they—like the crusades—are undertaken on the authority of the Church. An exalted moralism and an 'In God's name . . .' attitude ensure the rule of the good, and the extirpation of the bad lends ideological force to the violent prosecution of one's own interest, under the cover of the general well-being and of the will of God. The unbelievers and the heretics had no right to exist if they did not 'convert'. The Albigensian crusade (the first quarter of the thirteenth century)[18] emphasised the intermingling of divine and political motives, as was the case with the violent conversion of the Lithuanians by the knights of the Teutonic Order (fourteenth century).

A modern historian may ask in this regard whether it was a matter of orthodox belief or of power over people and land. The intermingling of the two motives means that they are inextricable in many cases. In every instance, there is little or no respect for the just concern of an opponent to defend his individual belief, conviction, culture, and territory. Not a blade remained in the face of the claims to power and truth of a theocratic way of thinking and acting. Freedom to extend the liturgy was not recognised as a moral value. Only uniformity in the one faith counted as the politico-ethical norm. Deviation from it could justify a war. People who thought differently were not treated with respect for their fundamental human rights, but were violently persuaded to adopt unity in truth.

5. ST THOMAS AQUINAS

As is known, Aquinas (1225–74) rejected the notion of a 'war of conversion', and looked on crusades—even in the form of an 'armed pilgrimage'—with mistrust. But he also thought that the most justifiable of wars was one undertaken by order of the Church against the enemies of papal authority and of Christians.

The criteria which he standardised for assessing the just nature of a war are as follows: 1. it is ordered on the authority of a lawful ruler; the war is waged for the sake of a just cause; 3. the intention of pursuing the war is to promote a good end.[20] These criteria bring together the ways of thinking proper to natural law and to Christian ethics. Aquinas followed Aristotle in acknowledging the natural grounding of the public authority of a government. A government has the task of helping a community to attain its natural goal, when the general good takes precedence over the individual good. The maintenance of peace is a fundamental condition for a good communal life, and the use of arms is permissible to ensure such a peace. That is a natural concern but also an activity which is pleasing to God. Not merely God's own people Israel, but every nation has received from God the right to defend its existence with weapons—thus Aegidius Romanus (c. 1245–1316).[21]

The Aristotelian natural order of thought, which also allowed that war could be a socially responsible activity, is, according to Aegidius, a divinely sanctioned order. Accordingly, the name of God is employed to abrogate all moral objections to the use of force. F. H. Russell says of this development in thinking about war: 'This divinisation of the teleology of the just war is the most extreme justification of warfare'. [22]

The consequences of this line of thought are clear. Every Christian national state must have possible recourse to the theologically sublimated principles of natural law in order to justify its wars.[23] The divine order and the national order largely coincide in this way of thinking. As the case law of a national state or regime would argue, an enemy is removed from the divine order. He is marked as a traitor and outlawed—banned from the territory of the state and treated as if he were also abandoned by God. Thus the practice of the national monarchies, but also of the small yet powerful Italian city states with many factions and disputes between noble and patrician families. The moralisation and divinisation of the case law of one party in the conflict is of the greatest possible assistance in mobilising one's own adherents. The secular wisdom of the Romans is thus obscured and a religious and moral fanaticism rules where sober judgment should be able to apportion matters justly in legal relations. The state of the modern period, whose monarchs are proclaimed as ruling by virtue of 'divine right', and more boldly even advertise themselves as 'God on earth',[24] find that the theory and theology of the just war provide them with an ideological weapon which has served more to legitimise than to moderate aggression and intolerance.

6. THE DIVISION OF CHRISTIANITY INTO WARRING FACTIONS

The theory of the just war in its complete form is a moral, religiously based doctrine of natural law, which establishes norms for the regulation of the use of force between states, and develops legal and statutory criteria in order to keep the actual conduct of war within the bounds of moral acceptability, and remove it from unarmed citizens, women and children—and priests and religious. But a range of questions remained unresolved: What authority is to control the mutual relations of states? How can one ensure an authoritative regulation of the moral conduct of war? Who is to establish guilt and to identify the unjust aggressor? Is there an entity that could assume so independent a position that it would remain totally uncompromised and impose obedience to itself?

In view of the lack of an internationally recognised and accepted legal procedure and of an authority which was competent to pass supra-national judgments, in the late Middle Ages it was often proposed that the pope or the 'world emperor' should act as the highest moral authority.[25] But in the fourteenth century the imperial structure became the plaything of the German princes. Moreover, in the fifteenth and sixteenth centuries the papacy compromised itself by wars against the emperor and the French king, in underhand and disloyal behaviour in regard to peace treaties and in secret pacts with the Turks when it seemed advisable for reasons of self-preservation. There was a constant identification of one's own concerns with those of God and a human sacrifice to imaginary advantage.

The moral superiority of one's own camp was enhanced in propaganda terms by portraying one's opponent as the devil incarnate. This was how the Byzantines described Western Christians, and *vice versa*. Latin and oriental Christians treated Islam—especially the Turks—similarly.[26] The image of the foe was consistently refined linguistically and pictorially in order to maintain moral tension in one's own ranks. Moral abuses in one's own camp were systematically overlooked to ensure a state of mobilisation.

Desiderius Erasmus (1469-1536) was also extremely suspicious of the moral superiority which Christians adopted in regard to the Turks, considering how Christian nations and princes behaved towards one another. The evangelical disposition of heart which he observed in so sorry a state in princes, soldiers, popes, bishops and cardinals had to be transformed universally into peace and harmony, and into respect for human freedom and justice. He drew the practical conclusion that it ought to be possible to substitute an evangelical attitude for readiness for war. Though he called the Turks a base and rapacious people, he thought Christians were no better. He believed that the conversion of unbelievers had to start with the banishment of 'the Turk' from one's own heart.[27]

7. RELIGIOUS PEACE AND RELIGIOUS WARS

With this evangelical and humanistic viewpoint, on the threshold of the New Age, Erasmus adopted a position which demanded acknowledgment of the enemy's fundamental attitude and a respectful estimate of the other's individuality. The transformation of bumptious moral superiority into evangelical humility requires people to lay down their weapons and devote themselves to prayer and to a reformation of moral behaviour in order to prove acceptable in the sight of God. For Erasmus, the theory of a 'just war' has become untenable in principle. Readiness for dialogue with another, even with one's opponent, is indicated, as Nicholas of Cusa also recommended in his treatise on peace in faith (*De Pace Fidei*).[28] Dialogue between Jews, Islam, and Byzantine and Latin Christians began in the fifteenth century in pursuit of a religious peace on the basis of general 'catholic' principles also recognised and approved in other traditions of belief.

The sixteenth century became instead the period of religious wars, when people of different persuasions, Catholics, Anabaptists, Huguenots, Lutherans and Calvinists, were driven from house and hearth. Opposing Christian churches and princes assumed separate control of religious truth and forced their opponents outside the bounds of national unity.

It remained for the Second Vatican Council to recognise religious freedom as a fundamental value in one and every society.

Translated by J. G. Cumming

Notes

1. *De civitate Dei* XIV, 1 (*Corpus Christianorum, Series Latina* 47, 48) (Turnhout 1955); *The City of God*, trans. Henry Bettenson (Harmondsworth 1972).

2. *Historia de duabus civitatibus* ed. W. Lammers (Darmstadt 1960) with German translation.

3. J. van Laarhoven *Récherches sur le concept 'Christianitas' pendant la réforme ecclésiastique de Grégoire VII jusqu'à Bernard* (Rome 1959).

4. *De officiis* I (II), cpa. 4, 8, 11–13; *De Republica* 3, cap. 23 35. Cf. S. Albert, *Bellum justum. Die Theorie des 'gerechten Krieges' und ihre praktische Bedeutung für die auswärtigen Auseinandersetzungen Roms in republikanischer Zeit* (Kallmunz 1980); Y. Garlan *War in the Ancient World* (London 1975).

5. *Ethica Nicomachea* X 7, 1177b 4. Cf *Politica* 1333 b38–1334a 2; 11, 1253 a 37; 1256 b 223–6.

6. The Book of Joshua on the conquest of the land of Canaan; Judges, 6–8 on Gideon; 1 and 2 Maccabees.

6. The Book of Joshua on the conquest of the land of Canaan; Judges, 6–8 on Gideon; 1 and 2 Maccabees.

7. Matt. 26:52; Rom. 12, 119; Heb. 10:330; Matt.5:39.

8. Rom. 13:4.

9. *Expositio* in Lc, X, 53 (*ad Rc* 22, 36, 38) Migne, PL, 15, 1817.— Letter to the Emperor Theodosius (346–95). Ep. 51, Migne, PL, 16, 1160–1164, *De obitu Theodosii oratio, ibid.*, 11396–7.

10. *De civitate Dei* (*The City of God*; cf. 1 above) XIX, 7.

11. Carl Erdmann *Die Entstehung des Kreuzgedankens* (Stuttgart 1935).

12. Benoit Lacroix 'Deux le veut! La theologie d'un cri' in *Etudes de la civilisation médiévale* (IXe–XIIe siecles. Mélanges offerts à Ecmond-René Labande (Poitiers 1974).

13. A selection from the recent literature in various major languages: Jean Guiraud *L'inquisition mediévale* (Paris 1978); Bartolome Bennassar *L'inquisition espagnole.* XVe–XIXe siècle (Paris 1979); Bernd Rill *Diese Inquisition und ihre Ketzer* (Puchheim 1982); Angel Alcala y otros *Inquisicion espanola y mentalidad inquisitorial: ponencias del simposio internacional sobrer inquisicion* (New York 1983) (Barcelona 1984); *The Inquisition in Early Modern Europe: Studies on Sources and Methods*, eds. Gustav Henningsen and John Tedeschi (DeKalb 1986).

14. See F. H. Russell *The Just War in the Middle Ages* (Cambridge 1975) pp. 40–212.

15. Russell *op. cit.* pp. 86–212.

16. *Ibid.* p. 129.

17. *Ibid.* p. 128.

18. F. Niel *Albigeois et Cathares* (Paris 1974).

19. T. G. Chase *The Story of Lithuania* (New York 1946); H. Beumann, 'Kreuzzugssgedanke und Ostpolitik im hohen Mittelalter' in *Historisches Jahrbuch* 72 (1953) 112–132; Manfred Hellmann, *Grudzuğe der Geschichte Litauens und des litauischen Volkes* (Darmstadt 1966); *The Lithuanian State of 1529* trans. and ed. Karl von Loewe (Leiden 1976).

20. *Summa Theologiae* IIa–IIae q. 40 art 1–3; Russell *op. cit.* pp. 258–91.

21. *De regimine principum* III, III, 23 (ed. Rome 1607) (rep. Aalen 1967) p. 623 et seq.; Russell *op. cit.* p. 266.

22. *Op. cit.* p. 266.

23. P. Contamine '*La guerre de Cent Ans* (Paris 1972–) p. 116.

24. A. G. Weiler *Deus in Terris. Middeleeuwse wortels van de totalitaire ideologie* (Hilversum 1965).

25. For instance by Dante Alighieri *De Monarchia* ed. G. Vinay (Florence 1950).

26. R. Schwoebel *The Shadow of the Crescent: The Renaissance Image of the Turk* [*1453–1517*] (New York 1967); J. W. Bohnstedt *The Infidel Scourge of God. The Turkish Menace as seen by German Pamphleteers of the Reformation Era* (Philadelphia 1968).

27. Erasmus *Utilissima Consultatio de Bello Turcis Inferendo*, obiter enarratus Psalmus XXV III, ed. A. G. Weiler in *Opera Omnia Erasmi* V–3 (Amsterdam 1986) pp. 1–82.

28. Nicholas of Cusa *De pace fidei, cum epistola ad Joannem de Segovia* ed. R. Klibansky and H. Bascour (Mediaeval and Renaissance Studies, Suppl. 3) (London 1956).

29. *Dignitatis humanae* (7 December 1965).

Michael Erbe

Charlemagne's Conquest of Saxony

THE SO-CALLED Frankish annals of the kingdom—a historical work which can be more or less regarded as official—announce for the year 785/6 the victory of Charlemagne (768–814) over the Saxons. He first spent the winter at the Eresburg (at Marsberg-on-the-Diemel, on the southern boundary of the Saxon tribal region) held, for the first time on Saxon territory, a royal assemly in Paderborn, and undertook from there several campaigns as far as what is today the Lüneburg Heath. His enterprises were crowned when his fiercest opponent Widukind submitted and was baptised. The annals close this year with the words: '*Et tunc tota Saxonia subiugata est*' ('and then the whole of Saxony was subjugated'). Even if there were still uprisings until 804, the war which began in 772 was now by and large over. The incorporation of Saxony into the extended Frankish kingdom was to be of undreamt-of importance for the future development of western Central Europe.

In many respects Saxony was an exception among the Germanic kingdoms of the early Middle Ages. Almost all the tribes from the time of the migration of the peoples had formed a military kingdom and, through contact with the Roman state, had attained certain forms of statehood. The Saxons on the other hand, who from the second century had pushed south from Schleswig-Holstein and had spread out between the Lower Rhine and the Elbe and Saale rivers as far as the southern foothills of the Harz mountains, as well as roughly to the line of the Diemel, Möhne and Ruhr rivers, formed a federally organised 'tribal state'. It seems that on the journey south, a not exclusively warlike affair was over by the end of the seventh century, this union was joined by several tribes, others being subjugated by force. This is reflected in the social organisation of the Saxons which has come down to us in sources dating from the 8th century. They speak fairly unanimously of *edlingen* or *nobiles*, of *frilingen* or *liberti* as well as of *lazzen* or *servi*. That is nobles, freedmen and serfs. Together with *nobiles* or *nobiliores* some sources give *liberi* or *Edelfreie* who can be identified with those Franks who could have been of help to the Saxons invading from the north in the conquest of the country. At all events, Saxons and Franks did not always fight with one another, but also gave one another political support. This can be seen for example in the joint suppression of the Kingdom of Thuringia in 531, in which its northerly part—the 'Nordthüringgau' between Unstrut, Saale and Harz—was acquired by the Saxons.

With the two less free social classes we seem to be dealing with members of subjugated tribes, in the case of the nobles with basically the ruling class of the conquering people and their warriors, but also in part with those tribes who came to terms with the advancing northeners. In this connection the name of one of the sub-groupings into which the sources divide the Saxons, stands out: together with the Westphalians and Eastphalians or East people are the Engern ('Angrarii') who probably in part go back to the Angrivariari, already mentioned by Tacitus as being in this area. In their territory was the assembly place Marklô (= 'frontier forest', probably close to present-day Marklohe near Nienburg on the Weser). This was where envoys met annually, twelve from each individual class from each of the districts, about 50 in all, into which the Saxon tribal union was divided. The assembly determined who was to head the individual districts, and without exception it was the members of the noble families who held office as *satrapae* or *praepositi*. In addition, the Westphalians, Engern and East Saxons each had, in time of war, a duke (*dux*) as army commandere. This district federal structure points to the fact that the Saxon tribal union was by no means a form of state founded exclusively on conquest and subjugation. Rather, in the various phases of its development—from the start of its expansion north of the Elbe until it reached its frontiers on the eve of the Carolingian era—it must have incorporated new ethnic units by conceding equal rights each time. But it was the federal character of the Saxons which made conquest and missionary work so difficult. It was not just a simple matter of subjugating a kingdom or a tribal dukedom or of Christianising a whole people by baptising a ruler as a respected central figure. What was needed were various attempts in different places until the incorporation of the Saxons into the Frankish kingdom and their acceptance of the new faith were achieved.

The decision to incorporate the Saxon tribal region into the Frankish kingdom was certainly not only religiously but also politically motivated. Under the Merovingians the Frankish kingship was seldom strong enough to form a real threat to its neighbours, and this despite the imposing extent of the Frankish kingdom. This changed when Charles Martel, Charlemagne's grandfather, as major-domo (714–741), united the entire political power of the kingdom in his hands. Above all he subjugated in 733–734 a large part of the Friesians' territory, that is the present-day Dutch provinces of Seeland, Holland and (West-) Friesland. But the main expansionist thrust was aimed further along the East Friesian coast of the North Sea, and it was to be supported by Christian missionary work helped by Anglo-Saxon monks, above all by Willbrord and Winfried-Bonifatius, the latter meeting his death in 754 at Dokkum, north-east of Leeuwarden. The stabilising of the Frankish kingdom, completed among other things with the support of the Church, also brought an increase in political pressure on the Saxons who were, in addition, threatened by encirclement in the north. It must also have been in the Frankish rulers' interest to incorporate Saxon territory in the strengthened kingdom, in order to achieve a more favourable frontier along the course of the Saale and Elbe, and to gain better control of the bordering territories of the Thuringian-Hessian area, on the Lower Rhine and on the North Sea coast. Christian missionary work was an important means of doing this. Together with that went the military actions undertaken on several occasions from 718 onwards by Charles Martel against the Saxons, above all in 738 when he mounted a highly effective campaign against the Westphalians, and also that of his son Pippin (741–768) against the East Saxons ten years later.

It seems as if it was from that time that the Christian missionary work took on the character of subjection and oppression in Saxon eyes. That applied above all to the western parts of the tribal region which were first exposed to the Frankish advances. Up till then the Saxons had by no means remained unaffected by missionary work, and this also seems to have already led to considerable successes. At least archaeological finds point in that direction: in the course of the seventh century there is a noticeable increase in the whole of Saxony in burial grounds where bodies are buried in an east-west direction, indicating Christian burial practice. While this tendency persists in eastern Saxony in the eighth century, this process is reversed in the North, and above all in the West during this period. Apparently political pressure led here to a return to the old religious customs.

As almost everywhere in the conversation of the Germanic tribes, missionary work probably began with an initial attempt to start at the 'political' top in order to achieve the baptism of the whole people. In Saxony that meant turning to the nobles at the head of the districts, the dukes leading the tribal sub-divisions, as well as to the annual assembly at Marklô. At the same time interference with or even killing of missionaries could well lead to complications with the Franks, so that the canvassers for the new religion were at first guaranteed a certain measure of security. When about 695 the 'two Ewalds' (missionaries about whom we otherwise know very little) were murdered in Saxony, the perpetrators were punished on Saxon territory itself. In the forties or fifties of the eighth century the Anglo-Saxon Lebuin went to Marklô to preach before the assembled Saxons. He was protected by friendly nobles from popular anger which could have lead to his being stoned. Everything points to the fact that, particularly among the nobles, there was a slow realisation that they could only preserve their independence from the Franks if they accepted Christianity and gave their powerful neighbours no reason for conquest by evading the work of the missionaries. It was only the powerful development of Frankish expansionist will under Charlemagne that led to a hardening of attitude and to a deeper consideration or even a rethinking of their own religion. About this religion, centred on a tree-trunk called 'Irminsul' and appearing to carry with it an idea of an all-embracing power, we know incidentally just as little as we know about individual religious customs. All kinds of magic, idolatry, prophecies and the like have been preserved in a text written down in the monastery at Fulda at the end of the 8th century. The ordinary people in particular seem to have clung to these for a long time. This stubborn resistance led in 785 to drastic regulations contained in the so-called *Capitulatio de partibus Saxoniae*. This provided, amongst other things, for the death penalty for violating Church peace, for attacking priests, for cremation, refusing baptism, sacrificing to heathen gods, but also for disloyalty to the king's people as well as for the murder of one's own master. This shows that it was primarily the upper class who supported the Franks. Every church had to have at its disposal a farm of two hides of land together with a man-servant and maid-servant.

As far as can be gathered from later conditions of ownership and patronage, and in addition from the saints to whom the churches were consecrated, the oldest houses of God originated as missionary cells and baptismal centres along the Frankish army routes and in the military bases set up at regular intervals along these routes. In addition, there were soon the personal churches of the nobility who co-operated with the Franks and who moreover made extensive gifts of land to monasteries in the neighbouring territory which were appointed to conduct the missionary work in Saxony. On this land more early churches were built from which the surrounding countryside was slowly Christianised. The most important monasteries for missionary work were Hersfeld as well as Fulda through its branches in Hamelin and Brunshausen near Gandersheim, Werden on the Ruhr with its branches in Helmstedt, and in the ninth century, Corvey and Herford as well, which were already new monastery foundations in Saxon territory.

It is surprising on the other hand that it was some time before bishoprics were established. The creation of a unified ecclesiastical province for the entire Saxon territory with an archbishop in perhaps Münster or Paderborn would also have been appropriate. Resistance by delaying tactics, which to the north of the Elbe could only be broken by resettlement of large sections of the population as far as the river Main, and in addition the initial scarcity of Saxon clerics, led to the Saxons being placed under the bishops of Cologne and Mainz who thereby were promoted to metropolitan. For their part, they set up missionary cells, whereby Paderborn (a bishopric since 806–807) was dependent on assistance from the cathedral school of Würzburg, Verden (810–814) on that from the monastery at Amorbach, Bremen (804–805) on people from Worms, Minden, Osnabrück and Münster (800–805) on help from Lüttich and Utrecht; and those bishoprics which were the last to be set up, Hildesheim (815) and Halberstadt (827) even received support from the ecclesiastical province of Rheims. Bremen, united in the meantime with Hamburg, was raised to archbishopric in 864, so that the Scandinavian missionary work could be conducted from there; Magdeburg, whose diocese was divided off from the bishopric of Halberstadt, received through Emperor Otto the Great (936–973) an archbishop for the conversion of the Slavs. This was a continuation of the example of Saxon missionary work.

Otto the Great did not do this by chance. He was after all a descendant of a family of high Saxon nobility who adapted to the Franks at the earliest opportunity, accepted Christianity and assisted in conversions: namely the 'Liudulfinger' from the area of Gandersheim, who put land at the disposal of Brunshausen which was Fulda's missionary monastery. The first member of this family we know about, Liudolf by name, died as a monk in the monastery of Fulda in 780. During the ninth century the family, which certainly belonged to the lineage of Saxon nobility who put the Franks instead of their own people at the head of the newly instituted earldoms, attained the title of duke in Saxony; in 919 their first representative, Duke Henry, became German king. At that time the land conquered by Charlemagne had become the central territory of the East Frankish-German Empire. During the tenth century the now Christianised territory became the base for further missionary work to the North and East.

Translated by Gordon Wood

Literature

Martin Lintzel: *Ausgewählte Schriften* Bd. 1: *Zur altsächsischen Stammesgeschichte* (Berlin 1961); Walther Lammers (ed.) *Entstehung und Verfassung des Sachsenstammes* (= Wege der Forschung, Bd. 50) (Darmstadt 1967). Michael Erbe: Studien zur Entwicklung des Niederkirchenwesens in Ostsachsen vom 8. bis zum 12. Jahrhundert (= *Veröffentlichungen des Max-Planck-Instituts für Geschichte* Bd. 26 *Studien zur Germania Sacra* Bd. 9) (Göttingen 1969); Walther Lammers (ed.), *Die Eingliederung der Sachsen ins Frankenreich* (= *Wege der Forschung* Bd. 135) (Darmstadt 1970).

Enrique Dussel

Was America Discovered or Invaded?

THE QUINCENTENARY of the arrival of Christopher Columbus in the West Indies in 1492 will soon be celebrated. In a spirit of triumphalism which is completely at odds with the historical facts, the Church has already started preparing for these celebrations at the highest level. On 11 February 1988, the *Asociación Indígena Salvadoreña* (Salvadoran Indian Association) published *I Encuentro espiritual y cultural* (Spiritual and Cultural Encounter I) in which it repudiated the foreign invasion of America and called a halt to the genocide and ethnocide of its peoples and cultures and also demanded a complete rejection of the celebration of 500 years of that *foreign invasion*.[1] The fact is that the first Europeans reached these lands towards the end of the fifteenth century—the Spaniards came first, followed by the Portuguese and then the Dutch, English, French, etc.; and it is claimed that they 'discovered' (they revealed what was covered) that these lands formed a continent. It is further claimed that they 'evangelised' the indigenous peoples of the continent. There is not much awareness of the fact that both of these terms already indicate an interpretation which con-ceals (which hides or covers over) the historical event. From the European point of view (from above), something was dis-covered; from the point of view of the inhabitants of the continent (from below), what we are really dealing with is an invasion by foreigners, by aliens, and by people from outside; people who murdered the menfolk, educated the orphans and went to bed with ('lived with' was the sixteenth century Spanish euphemism) Indian women. 'After killing off all those who wanted, yearned for or even thought about liberty, or to be relieved of the torments they suffered, as all *native leaders and adult males*

126

did (because they normally allow only youngsters and women to survive these war)', then those who are left alive are 'subjected to the hardest, most horrific and harshest servitude that man or beast could ever endure'.[2]

1. THE INVENTION OF AMERICA

Incredible as it may seem, it is now more than 30 years since the historian Edmundo O'Gorman presented the thesis which became the title of his famous book *La invención de América* (The Invention of America).[3] Inspired by Heidegger, his thesis is a masterly ontological analysis which far exceeds the limits of perfunctory anecdotal material. Taking as a point of departure the European concept of 'being in the world' of the likes of Columbus or of Amerigo Vespucio, then the notional 'American being' is generated from the idea of 'Asian being' since the islands of the Caribbean were understood to be properly situated in the great ocean adjacent to the continent of Asia, just like the archipelagos of Japan or of the Philippines. As far as Europe was concerned, there only existed Africa to the south and Asia to the east. America simply was not there. 'When it is claimed', writes O'Gorman, 'that America was invented, we are dealing with an attempt to explain a *being* (*Dasein*) whose existence depends on the way that it is understood by Western culture. The coming into being of America is an event that depends on the form of its appearance.'[4] Accordingly Western culture has the 'creative capacity of giving its own existence to a being which that culture understands to be different and alien'.[5]

This vision which to a certain extent is creative *ex nihilo* of being or of the meaning of entity is the way in which many historians conceive what is essentially South American; this also applies to Church history. The native American was seen as a mere material being, devoid of feeling, of history and of humanity—even his name, 'Indian', was of Asian origin since it was believed that he was a Hindu from India; he was merely a potential *recipient* of evangelisation who could not and was not expected to make any contribution of any kind—an invented non-being. This is an extreme, euro-centric point of view which has, nevertheless, been postulated by a South American historian—an extraordinarily absurd piece of self-deception!

2. THE DIS-COVERY OF AMERICA

Theologically, dis-covery seems at least slightly more positive to an American than mere invention. Dis-covery at least presumes the prior existence of something which was covered and was not created from a vacuum. However, the use of the term 'dis-cover' implies that the point of departure in this process is the European ego which is a constituent element of the historical event: 'I discover', 'I conquer', 'I evangelise' (in the missionary sense) and 'I think' (in the ontological sense). The European ego turns the newly dis-covered primitive native into a mere object—a thing which acquires meaning only when it enters the world of the European. Fernández de Oviedo wondered if native Americans were even human and he stated: 'These people of the (West) Indies, although rational and of the same race as those of the holy ark of Noah have become irrational and bestial because of their idolatries, sacrifices and devilish ceremonies'.[6] Thus, the European ego (of conquistador, missionary or merchant) considered the other as something which only acquired meaning because it had been dis-covered (revealed): what it had already been was of no consequence.

Accordingly, any discussion about dis-covery inevitably limits parameters to *one* perspective which is incomplete, is in favour of those who dominate and is from above. In the same way, mission or evangelisation, the basic activity of the missionary, only takes into account the ecclesial ego which, along with the conquistador from Spain or the merchant from Holland or England, preaches the doctrines of Christianity to the newly dis-covered 'for the greater glory of God' (*ad maiorem Dei gloriam*).

Nearly every history of the Church describes events in the mission areas of South America, Africa and Asia from the sixteenth to the end of the nineteenth century as a glorious expansion of Christianity. As Hegel stated: 'Europe became the missionary agent for civilisation throughout the world'.[7] In this process, one has to note both the deification of civilisation and the secularisation of mission; in fact, both amount to the same thing and euro-centralism is basic to both.

3. FOREIGN INVASION (A COPERNICAN UPSET FOR AMERICAN SUBJECTIVITY)

The notions of invention and dis-covery, as well as those of conquest and evangelisation are centred on Europeans as constituent egos. But if we take a Copernican leap and abandon our accepted world view of the European ego to look around and try to understand things from the perspective of the primitive American native where the American Indian ego becomes the core of this new solar system, everything takes on a new significance (from below). Tupac Amaru was an Inca and a rebel; he was put to death by being pulled apart by four horses at Cuzco in Peru in 1781 because he had tried to gain freedom for his own oppressed Indian people. In a statement found in his pocket when he was imprisoned, he wrote: 'For that reason, and because of the voices which have cried to Heaven' (as in Exodus),[8] 'in the name of the Almighty God, we ordain and order, that not one of these said people, render any payment to or obey in any way these intruding European agents'.[9]

The word 'intrusion', from the latin *intrusio* (a violent entering), means an entry into someone else's world which is uninvited and without permission. Amaru, a great rebel and popular liberation theologian,[10] saw Europeans as intruders into our continent; intruders who had invaded, occupied, and taken over a particular space: the space in which the world, the culture, the religion and the history of American man belonged. Faced with the unfamiliar European, the first reaction of the native inhabitant was one of bewilderment: an inability to know what to think or what to do. As has already been pointed out, the native American was given the Asian misnomer Indian which had no bearing on his world; and, within terms of that world, his only natural solution to the extraordinary problem of his encounter with Europeans, with their fair skin and fair hair, with their horses and dogs which he had never seen before, with their cannons and gunpowder and their metal armour, was to see them as gods: 'They really inspired fear when they arrived. Their faces were so unfamiliar. The Mayans took them to be gods. Tunatiuh[11] slept in the house of Tzumpam'.[12]

The emperor Montezuma of Mexico experienced the same wonder when he met the invader Hernán Cortés, since 'having already consulted his own people', as José de Acosta writes, 'they all assured him that without doubt his ancient and great master Quezalcoatl[13] had returned as he said he would and that that was why he had come from the East'.[14] The aboriginal American neither invented nor dis-covered the new arrivals. He admired them with a sacred respect as they invaded his land; he found his own understanding for them which was quite different from that of the European invaders. At first, Europeans interpreted what they found in terms of an Asian being and then in terms of an American being when it was understood that America formed a fourth part of the known world along with Europe, Africa and Asia. The invaders were understood with the same kind of limitations by the native Americans[15] who saw them as gods who had appeared amongst them. This understanding, in its turn, demanded answers to such questions as why the divine beings had come, whether they had come to demand their rights and to punish or whether they had come to bless and endow. This initial encounter created feelings of expectation, of unease, of admiration:

'The admiral and others noted their simplicity—as Bartholomé de las Casas told us on 12 October 1492—and how they took great pleasure in and enjoyed everything; the Spaniards took careful note of the Indians (sic) and how much gentleness, simplicity and trust they showed towards people they had never seen. They seemed to have returned to a state of innocence such that it seemed a matter of a mere six hours or so since our common father Adam himself had lived'.[16]

4. THE VISION OF THOSE WHO WERE CONQUERED (A DESTROYED SUBJECTIVITY)

The original face-to-face encounter did not last very long and the American Indians soon discovered why these gods had come: 'They soon found out what they were really like and that they were the most cruel and hungry wolves, tigers and lions who threw themselves at them. For the last forty years and including this very day, they have done nothing but tear them apart, kill them off, cause them distress, hurt them, torment them and destroy them by every conceivable and unimaginable form of cruelty'.[17]

In actual fact, from within his own world, the native American lived in great terror through the invasion by these divine beings: 'Ahuau Katún 11[18] the first one in the story, is the original katún . . . it was during this katún that the red-bearded foreigners, the children of the sun, the fair skinned ones, arrived. Woe! Let us lament because they arrived! They came from the east, these messengers of the sign of the divinity, these foreigners of the earth. Woe! Let us lament because they came, the great builders of stone piles;[19] the false gods of the earth who can make fire burst from the ends of their arms.[20] 'Woe! Heavy is the weight of the katún in which Christianity first appears! This is what is going to happen: there will be an enslaving power, men will become slaves, a slavery that will include even the Chiefs of the Thrones'.[21] 'The hearts of the Lords of the people will tremble and be full of fear because of the signs of this katún: an empire of war, an epoch of war, words of war, food of war, drink of war, a journey of war, a government of war. It will be a time for old men and old women to wage war, for children and brave men to wage war, for young men to wage war on behalf of our honoured gods'.[22]

This glorious conquest and even the accompanying evangelisation will always be closely linked to that perverse ethical activity: a generative evil and a structural oppression which still weigh so heavily on our lives even as we approach the end of the twentieth century. Accordingly, the original inhabitants, within terms of their own world, had a very personal perception of the events which followed the discovery. The world of the foreign oppressor saw things in terms of a discovery *cum* conquest while within our subjective American world it was a process of bewilderment, servitude and death. The same events, therefore, generated two quite different sets of feelings and effects.

5. THE CREATIVE RECEPTION OF THE GOSPEL AND AN HISTORICAL INDEMNIFICATION

In his Testament (1564), Bartolomé has written an explicit piece of liberation theology:

> 'God saw fit to choose me to try to make good to all these peoples we call Indians, owners of these countries and lands, some of the insults, the wrongs and the injuries of a kind unseen and unheard of, which, contrary to all reason and justice, they have received at the hands of us Spaniards, to restore them to their *first liberty* of which they have been so unjustly deprived and to *liberate them* from the violent death they still suffer'.[23]

'These peoples'—the Indians—were free and were masters of these lands. They were invaded and dispossessed, oppressed and impoverished. However, they did get the Gospel message, even if that occurred frequently in spite of the missionaries. Christ crucified and bleeding (more a feature of the South American baroque style than of the contemporary Spanish style),[24] made the Indians aware of their identity with the Son who had been put to death. They lived out in their own bodies, in their complete poverty, in their absolute nakedness, impoverished in the fullest sense of the word, the cross which the missionaries preached about. It was no mere passive apprenticeship or a learning by rote of Christian doctrine by those who had been conquered, but a creative acceptance of the Gospel from below. Can the fifth centenary of that kind of evangelisation be properly celebrated? Would that not be yet another insult of the kind indicated by Bartolomé de las Casas?

The word insult implies an offence against the honour and reputation of someone's rights. In actual fact, the dis-covery and the conquest were not only insults but forms of practical oppression and structured servitude, involving the killing off of a people and the destruction of a culture and a religion. The process involved more than insult; it was an offence, a humiliation, an assassination and the gravest sin against the dignity of others.

For these reasons, what has to occur in 1992 is an *historical indemnification* made to the American Indians. Although, I do believe that the one great protagonist who will be absent from the preparations for the commemoration of 12 October 1492 will be the *Indian himself*.

Indemnification surely involves, at the very least and even if it is so late, the making good of the offence committed against another person, fully satisfying the humiliated party and making compensation for the prejudice which has been inflicted. Can we do that? Is it too idealistic to restore all that has been taken away from the Indian? How can indemnification be made for the irreparable damage which has been done and is still being done?

In any case, the American Indian was never conquered. Hundreds of rebellions occurred during the period of colonial rule from the sixteenth to the nineteenth century and nowadays revolt is occurring in the struggles of the 'Second Emancipation',[25] in the *processes of liberation* being lived out at this very time in Guatemala, in El Salvador and in Nicaragua and in the whole of South America, wherever there is any problem or suffering. With Mariátegui[26] I believe that the Indian problem is most closely linked with the future of South America. An *historical indemnification* in 1992 would be a sign, a milestone on the road towards the Kingdom, leading to the freedom of the Indian in a liberated South America. A clear awareness of all this can come to us only from an historical conspectus which emerges from below.

Translated by John Angus Macdonald

Notes

1. See *El Día* (Mexico, 12 February 1988) p. 6. On the theme of 'discovery', see P. Chaunu *Conquête et exploitation des Nouveaux Mondes* (Paris 1977); E. Schmitt ed. *Die grossen Entdeckungen* (Munich 1984); I. P. Maguidovich *Historia del descubrimiento y exploración de Latinoamérica* (Moscow 1972); Z. Todorov *The Conquest of America* (New York 1985) in which my own hypothesis of viewing the Indian as 'other' is taken up in a levinasian theory which I first postulated in 1972.

2. See E. Dussel *Filosofía ética de la liberación* (Buenos Aires 1987) vol. 1 p. 5. For further explanation of this text see my own articles: 'Histoire de la foi chrétienne et changement sociale en Amèrique Latine' *Les luttes de liberation bousculent la théologie* (Paris 1975) pp. 39–99; 'Expansion de la cristiandad y su crisis' *Concilium* 164 (1981) pp. 80–89. For general information about the period see my 'Introducción General' to the colonial period in *Historia General de la Iglesia en América Latina* (Salamanca 1983) and *History of the Church in Latin America* (Grand Rapids 1981).

3. *FCE* Mexico 1957.

4. *Ibid.* p. 91.

5. *Ibid.* p. 97.

6. See E. Dussel 'La cristiandad moderna ante el otro' *Concilium* 150 (1979) p. 499.

7. See E. Dussel 'One Ethic and Many Moralities' *Concilium* 170 (1981) pp. 54–55.

8. See E. Dussel 'Paradigma del Exodo en la teología de la liberación', *Concilium* 209 (1987) pp. 99–114.

9. B. Lewis *La rebelión de Tupac Amaru* (Buenos Aires 1967) p. 421. For information about other Indian rebellions see J. Golte *Repartos y rebeliones* (Lima 1980); S. M. Yañez *Sublevaciones indígenas en la Audiencia de Quito* (Quito 1978); M. T. Huerta and P. Palacios *Rebeliones indigenas de la epoca colonial* (Mexico 1976).

10. See E. Dussel *Hipótesis para una historia de la teología en América Latina* (Bogota 1986) p. 33.

11. In the Mayan language 'tunatiuh' means the Sun God. They gave this name to the Spanish conquistador Álvarado, a brutal fair-haired soldier whose locks were taken by the natives to be the very rays of the sun.

12. See *Memorial de Sololá. Anales de los Cakchiqueles* 11, 148 (Mexico 1950) p. 126; N. Wachtel *La vision des vaincus. Les Indiens du Perou devant la Conquête espagnole* (Paris 1971); On American religions see W. Krickeberg, H. Trimborn, W. Mueller and O. Zerries *Die Religionen des Alten Amerika* (Stuttgart 1961); also M. L. Portillo *El reverso de la conquista* (Mexico 1964); F. Mires *En nombre de la cruz* (San Jose 1986) includes very fine piece of writing 'Discusiones teológicas y políticas frente al holocausto de los indios (periodo de conquista)'; S. Zavala *Filosofía de la conquista* (Mexico 1977); J. O. Beozzo 'Visão indigena da conquista e da evangelizacão', *Inculturacão e libertacão* (Sao Paulo 1986) pp. 79–116.

13. A 'god' of the peoples ruled over by the Aztecs (like the Greek Zeus vis a vis the Romans). The overlord had a 'bad conscience' and believed that the god of the underlings was coming to take his revenge for the oppression of his faithful. Cortés left from Tlaxcala, from the temple where Quezalcoatl was adored; the name means the 'divine duality' or 'the feathered serpent'; *coatl* means dualism and *quezal* refers to the splendid feathers of the quetzal bird which was itself a sign of the divinity.

14. *Historia Natural* vol. VII; Chap. 16; (Madrid 1954) p. 277.

15. Even the name 'American' is foreign and dominating and properly belongs to an Italian geographer and not to an 'American' as such'.

16. *Historia de las Indias* vol. L. Chap. 40 (Madrid 1957) p. 142.

17. B. de las Casas *Brevisima relacion de la destruccion de las Indias; ibid.* p. 137.

18. The proper name for an epoch, a 'kairos' of fear.

19. The reference is to the Spaniards' building of Churches in the sixteenth century.

20. *El libro de los libros de Chilam Balam* Part II. (Mexico 1948) pp. 124–125. The reference is to gunpowder and shotguns used by the Spaniards.

21. *Ibid.* p. 126.

22. *Ibid.* p. 137.

23. See *Obras* op. cit. p. 539.

24. See E. Dussel 'L'art chrètien de l'oprimé en Amérique Latine. Hypotèse pour caractériser une esthétique de la liberation' *Concilium* 152 (1980) pp. 55–70.

25. The 'First Emancipation' took place against Spain and Portugal from 1809. The 'Second Emancipation' began in 1959, but today the neocolonial metropolises are the industrialised countries on the 'centre'.

26. See his *Siete ensayos sobre la realidad peruana* (Lima 1954).

Herman Obdeijn

Christendom and Colonisation in Africa in the Nineteenth and Twentieth Centuries

1. THE POLITICAL DIVISION

IN THE course of the nineteenth century Europe became increasingly interested in the regions of Africa. Explorers mapped out the continent, trade agents displayed intensive activity, politicians showed interest in strategic positioning and spreading their influence, and the churches recognised a new field for their conversion activities. The result was, in both Protestant and Catholic circles, that numerous missionaries were sent out to Africa with the aim of spreading the Christian faith there.

These evangelists were the very first representatives of the Western world in many parts of Africa. During the whole of the nineteenth century they were frequently active in areas where European political or economic influence had not yet—or hardly—penetrated. One can safely say that they were the most important group of Europeans both in number and in regard to the intensity of contact with the population in the interior of Africa from 1850 to 1914.

Missionaries were children of their time and surroundings. They experienced their faith in the context of Western society and it was thus inevitable that they should bring their preconceived ideas with them along with the message of salvation as to the sort of community there should be within which the new faith was to be lived and practised.

Their influence therefore stretched out, not only to the concepts of faith

135

and practice but also to the political, social and economic circumstances in the areas where they were active. Conversion and the spread of civilisation were to go hand in hand; and by civilisation was understood: peace and calm, the introduction of trade based on a financial economy, and in fact the establishment of a community which was to be a reflection of that which obtained in Europe of the nineteenth century.

At first many missionaries hoped for a gradual reformation of African society without political interference from Europe. The Protestant Niger Mission in Nigeria with the help of former negro slaves from Sierra Leone; similar attempts in Kenya; initiatives in the direction of a theocratic community life on the shores of Lake Tanganyika under the auspices of the White Fathers, and, in Nyasaland, under the influence of Scottish missionaries—there are so many examples of attempts at Christianisation outwith the framework of colonialism.[1] It was only after 1880 that a change took place in the approach: the european missionary staffs became more pessimistic or more racist in their attitude towards their African helpers and the conviction grew that the resistance of unwilling and tyrannical princes could only be broken with the aid of a European colonial power. Although missionaries had not come with any preconceived political ambitions, they nevertheless in practice frequently played a role in the establishment of colonial authority.

Missionaries saw peace and order as prerequisites for their conversion activities; and this peace and order could in their view be assured only by European powers. A missionary in Kenya concluded: 'Where the might of a Christian nation is no longer evident, that is the limit set by Providence for the work of conversion'.[2] There are examples in plenty of situations where missionaries actively contributed to the establishment of colonial rule. In many cases this was in relation to their own country of origin, but not always: the French founder of the White Fathers, Cardinal Lavigerie, tried to arouse German interest in Uganda and the French missionary Coillard acted as intermediary in the spread of British influence in Rhodesia. In all of this they considered that, at the end of the day, they were serving the interests of the native population.

2. THE INFLUENCE ON THE AFRICAN COMMUNITY

Regarded from the perspectives of today many of the missionary initiatives look somewhat paternalistic. At the mission post of the White Fathers in German East Africa, for example, the Christians had to perform a number of tasks in the plantations but, according to the missionaries, this was intended to accustom them to the idea of regular work. Nor was the yoke applied by the Scottish missionaries and their successors in Nyassa always a light one.

It should be noted that the missionaries were often the first to express criticism when, in their opinion, the interests of the African population were not being protected, as for example in the Congo Free state of Leopold II. The colonial authorities tried to influence the independent stand taken by the missionaries by conceding them privileges and by demanding that as many missionaries as possible should originate from the country of the particular colonial administrative power. In the German areas and in the Belgian Congo this led to practically homogeneous groups of German and Belgian personnel. In Uganda the British Mill Hill fathers were brought in as a counter-balance to the white Fathers of French origin.

The activity of the missions had a deep effect on the traditional communites. In particular, they occupied an important place in the field of education. In the Belgian Congo and in many British areas they practically held the monopoly. Many missionaries saw education as one of the most effective means available to aid their work of conversion; and this was certainly the case where the reading of the Bible occupied a central position.

For the secular authorities, however, it meant at the same time a valuable contribution to the spread of their influence. The missions supplied a capable and reliable middle management for colonial rule and, at the insistence of the colonial authorities, an extensive place was made in the educational scene for the language, culture and history of the respective colonial power.[3] Christian values and norms as experienced in a European context were imposed on the African population as a matter of course.

Membership of the Church often had social and economic consequences for the Africans. Christianity brought a new social mobility—with all the consequences of this. The bonds of the new religious community sometimes proved stronger than tribal bonds and newly converted Christians were all the sooner prepared to cooperate with the colonial authorities. The individual family unit received greater emphasis than the family in a broader sense. Polygamy became an obstacle to those wishing to receive baptism.

In the introduction of modern agricultural and cattle breeding techniques missionaries played a role. Mission stations were often a sort of 'model farm' which had a powerful effect on surrounding areas.

3. THE 'PESTIS TETERRIMA' AND THE ENCYCLICAL 'MAXIMUM ILLUD'

Mission work and colonial politics in the twentieth century were, for all sorts of practical reasons, narrowly tied up with each other. Not everyone was blind to the dangers which accompanied this state of affairs. This became evident for example when, during the first World War, all the German missionaries in the German African colonies were interned. In the encyclical *Maximum illud* of 1919 Pope Benedict XV pointed out the danger of allowing too close an association between colonialism and Christianity. He spoke about a *pestis teterrima*. The missionary was called upon to forget his fatherland and commit himself completely to the work of the Church.

Furthermore, emphasis was laid on the formation of a native clergy—something which had till then received scant attention. In this connection there will certainly have been some prejudice concerning the quality of those of African descent. In the encyclical *Rerum ecclesiae* (1926) this instruction was again emphasised. Rome had probably been warned by the Russian revolution and the upsurge of nationalism, specifically in Asia. The pope made it clear that the native clergy would be called upon to govern their own church. Perhaps Rome was more far-sighted. But the missionaries in the field were often of another opinion: 'they' (the native clergy) could not yet be entrusted with real responsibility. Farther L. Leloir wrote, even in 1939: 'Where there is equal development—and often the native priest, though he be most pious and industrious, has not yet attained the general development of the white priest—the latter possesses nevertheless, over and above that of the native priest, the prestige of his race, his relations and the aureole of the great sacrifice that he made in coming so far to devote his life to his apostolate.[5] The nomination of two black bishops by Rome in 1938 was by no means welcomed by all.

4. MISSION AND NATIONALISM

The new Christians did not always prove as obedient as the missionaries would have desired. The Protestant missions in particular were confronted by developments which led to independent African Church communities which not only had a religious significance but also became a social factor of importance and in this way also the basis of various nationalist movements. In Catholic circles the upsurge of nationalist movements was looked upon with suspicion and African priests were forbidden to develop any activities along these lines.

The influential Bishop of Katanga in the Belgian Congo, Jean de Hemptinne, was one of the most outspoken antagonists of the Methodist preacher Simon Kibangu, who wanted to establish his own church. It was on the insistence of the mission which, along with other factors, caused Kibangu's imprisonment from 1921 until his death in 1951.

It cannot of course be denied that the missions contributed much to the formation of the new Africa. Most of the intellectual and nationalist leaders were moulded in missionary schools. But in general the European mission staffs had little admiration for the singularity of African culture. Church buildings were copies of village churches in Europe, the liturgy was still celebrated in latin, and the theological moulding of the young clergy was directed by the hand of Thomas Aquinas. When Father Tempels published, in 1945, his *Bantu Philosophy*, Bishop de Hemptinne saw to it that he was removed from the Congo.[6]

When, after the second World War, it became clear to many that times had changed and that the Africans wanted to take their destiny into their own hands, many missionaries found this difficult to accept and were of the opinion that things were changing too fast. In general the sense of really was sufficient for the inevitable to be accepted. Not everywhere however. The missions in the Belgian Congo stood rockfast behind the colonial authorities, who at that time would not budge an inch. It was not for nothing that Church and State there had been so intertwined since the Concordat of 1906. In the Portuguese colonies too, Church and State formed one body and only the White Fathers, in Mozambique in 1971, had the courage to show their solidarity with the independence movement. After all, in South Africa the Protestant Boers defended Apartheid in the name of the Bible; and, in Kenya, the European colonist pressed the British government in 1950 to make it clear to all that the British regime in Kenya would remain as builders of Christian civilisation.[7]

It must be said that the churches in many places chose to side with the nationalist leaders, of whom after all many were their pupils. Rome appointed African bishops at a brisk pace; and, ironically, the same missionaries who had seen the arrival of the colonial rulers now saw them depart—while they themselves were able in many places to maintain their positions albeit in altered circumstances.

5. AFTER INDEPENDENCE

After independence there was still tension between the new leaders and the Christian churches. Many white missionaries found it difficult to accept their new position: one in which they were no longer looked upon as a matter of course as the uncrowned heads of whole areas. Their departure and the reduced intake of new appointments from Europe, paved the way for an ever greater share in the leadership of the Church among the native clergy.

This new leadership was probably also better qualified to offer resistance to the dictatorial tendencies of certain political leaders. In countries such as the Congo/Zaire, Guinea, Ruwanda, and Uganda, conflict was sometimes violent. Catholics in particular were reproached for still thinking too much in colonial European terms. Some leaders maintained that, after colonialism, Christianity too would have to disappear since it was a 'foreign body' within the African community.

These tensions have also however had a purifying effect. African Christendom is now more adult and aware. In theology, in the liturgy and in cultural expression, authentic African values have found their place. The missionaries who are still there are no longer the people who set out how a Church service is to be, but rather are becoming the servants of the African Church—however difficult that has been for many of them.

Translated by Frank Carroll

Notes

1. See H. L. M. Obdeijn *The Political Role of Catholic and Protestant Missions in the Colonial Partition of Black Africa. A Bibliographical Essay* (Leiden 1983).

2. R. W. Strayer *The Making of Mission Communities in East-Africa. Anglicans and Africans in Colonial Kenya, 1875–1935* (London 1978, 33).

3. See, for example, A. W. Tiberondwa *Missionary Teachers as Agents of Colonialism. A study of their Activities in Uganda 1877–1925.* (Lusaka 1978).

4. J. J. de Wolf 'Sociaal-economische aspecten van de involved van de katholieke missie in Oost-Afrika' in J. M. Schoffeleers ed. *Missie en Ontwikkeling in Oost-Afrika* (Nijmegen-Baarn 1983) 40–53.

5. Quoted in André Picciola *Missionnaires en Afrique 1840–1940* (Paris 1987) 190.

6. See Adrian Hastings *A History of African Christianity 1950–1975* (London 1979) 63.

7. Hastings *op cit.* 24.

PART IV

Concluding Article

Ottmar John

The Tradition of the Oppressed as the Main Topic of a Theological Hermeneutics

1. A POLITICO-THEOLOGICAL FORMULATION OF THE HERMENEUTICAL PROBLEM

THE INTERPRETATION of texts from scripture and from ecclesiastical tradition is necessary whenever the text as it stands is no longer understood in the modern era. Interpretation has to mediate between two periods, between two contexts of thought which have become different from one another, and between two distinct social situations. In other words, interpretation derives from a specific difference between an existential and social situation and the event of revelation.

This difference, however, cannot be simply assigned to a formal and quantitative chronological and topographical difference. Neither measures of distance nor numbers of years separating the present moment from the saving event provide an adequate explanation of this difference. It has to be understood qualitatively. In order to assess correctly the difference between present-day western industrial societies with their bourgeois formation, with societies of Jesus' time, we have to look closely at the contemporary subjects of exegesis and their historical and social nature.

The incomprehensibility of the biblical texts and therefore any urge to mediate and interpret them are—so it is claimed—unique to bourgeois-capitalist societies. Such characteristics are associated with a concept of the subject which was formulated for the first time in the Enlightenment: that is, that the subject is that person who is conscious of his or her potentialities and abilities, and who knows that he or she is personally responsible for self, and for the existence of that self; hence, that he or she is independent and mature.

This self-awareness of autonomy and freedom[1] was derived from and developed as a consequence of the finding that without autonomy and freedom there can be no true knowledge and no moral activity. At the same time this self-awareness of autonomy has to be do with the material ability of at least some people to be actually and factually in the right position for, and to possess the means for, this national liberty. The Kantian identification of 'ought' with 'can' became effectively plausible only because the rise of enlightened bourgeois self-consciousness ushered in a considerable increase of economic and—especially in France—of political power.

On the one hand, the possession of economic means and the resulting power may be seen as prerequisites of any ability of human beings to conceive themselves as autonomous and free. On the other hand, the possession of economic means may also derive from a new relationship with the phenomenal world. Only an individual that understands self as an independently cognitive subject is in a position to use things as means for the extension of power, or to change material objects into such means, so that they ensure not solely the mere reproduction of life, but are appropriate to the acquisition of riches and power. In other words, only the autonomous subject is in a position to transform things into means of production: into means which multiply themselves, and take themselves as their very purpose.

But this is not the context in which to decide whether a materialist or an idealist interpretation is appropriate to the factual origin of modern autonomy. It is important, however, to realise that within the bounds of practical hermeneutics the exegetical subject is not just any individual that in earlier ages would have tried to use the same perceptual and cognitive structure to discern the word of God. Rather, the subject in capitalist societies has a specific autonomy which exists in the conscious mind, but a practical autonomy which forms and determines social conditions.

In other words, in capitalism the individual is constructed as an autonomous subject because he or she appropriates means, does something, and exercises power over nature and other people. Autonomous subjects, that is, the socially powerful class of autonomous individuals, use the acquisition of means in order to shape relations between human beings.

The autonomous subject is not autonomous merely by breaking with, and by liberation from, the rule of church authority and tradition, but essentially because, for the sake of self, the subject now independently determines the relations of human beings among themselves and to the past.[2]

In this regard, autonomy does not mean criticism or destruction of feudal rule, but power *per se ipsum* which is in a position to abrogate, establish and essentially mould circumstances. Therefore autonomy is the fundamental characteristic and condition for the exercise of rule under capitalism.

This historically novel autonomous subject embodies above all the bourgeois type. Autonomy, that very concept which enables the individual to constitute self in accordance with the unique specificity which allows of being subject at all, grossly contradicts experiences and traditions which see life and existence as a subject as gift and grace, and therefore as circumstances made possible from without.[3] Someone who directs his or her own life and uses his or her own means to wage the struggle, no longer sees any reason to hope in the redemption announced and promised in Scripture. For such persons the news of God's saving entry into history is relativised by the awareness that they have helped themselves.

This specific difference of the currently dominant form of self-consciousness from that proper to the promise of revelation is marked by the concept of economic power and autonomy. That tells us something about the size of the complex of problems regarding mediation and interpretation.

We must also remember that the central question which any interpretation of the biblical message has to face is a problem manufactured by politics and economics. Not everyone can adapt the meaning of texts and manipulate them to justify his or her own situation. That is possible only for those with the power and means to produce by themselves their own relationship to a past event and to its textual expression, and essentially to remould it in accordance with their own interests. In other words, an inaccurate, indeed phoney, result of a process of interpretation is always due to the asymmetry or overall imprecision of the particular way in which the present relates to the past. The danger of adapting God's free gift in revelation to human demands is therefore a danger which really threatens those with the power and means to satisfy their own needs.

To back texts with something alien and external to them, to read it into them so that it looks as if it is their very content, is possible only for those who possess something which is their own; something which is dependent on them alone and not made possible from without (by, say, the events which the texts in question describe). To justify power and domination by referring to and by interpreting texts from the past is not a universal human vulgarity which every individual commits when dealing with texts, but a methodological orientation on the part of those who have power and who rule.

Present-day interpreters of texts exercise power and autonomously relate to texts about past events, by means of two—ideally speaking—describable procedures: the selection and reductive exegesis of the contents of biblical texts; and their rehandling so as to objectify and aestheticise them.

There is a distinction to be made, so it seems, between the comprehensibility and the normative validity of the content of biblical and traditional faith. Even though certain aspects of content no longer seem comprehensible nowadays, its normative validity can be retained or the present age. Incomprehensible texts can unsettle and disturb dominant ideological models. On the other hand, a certain 'understating' of texts is possible which has no effect on present behaviour, being incapable either of orientation or of transforming it.

Theologians have tried and still try to approximate the biblical to the modern bourgeois framework of understanding by means of appropriate selection and construction. The first stage of historicist 'Life of Jesus' studies is a good example of this. The miracle stories which had become unacceptable to modern sensibility, the Son-of-God theology of the New Testament, the resurrection message, and so on, were sacrificed for the sake of an historically precise reconstruction of the actual life of Jesus—as, so to speak, 'it really was'. Only that part which was appropriate to the framework of a modern, scientifically-grounded notion of reality was acceptable as fact, as events which had actually happened. As Hartley says, the objective reality of events is ascertainable only in so far as they accord with the general conditions of the perception of actual reality as distinct from mere notional reality, and in so far as they can be included in an experimental context which has proved unexceptional hitherto.[4] The dominant modern orientation to facts subjects the Gospel message to an external criterion originating in the present moment. Hence what is chosen is what remains comprehensible today, and thus alone can claim to be valid.[5]

The incomprehensible parts of the message are then either wholly discarded (Jesusology!), or an abstraction is offered of their specific content, so that they are treated as relative 'means of expressing' something else, something specific. The incomprehensible passages are perceived as an image of the world or as a cultural framework which is conditioned by time and therefore is not normative.[6] Their 'pure' or 'genuine' meaning is distilled during the process of interpretation. In the process of demythologisation, therefore, the apocalyptic perception of time and disaster became a mere eschatology of the present moment, which everyone could already acquire in their existential decision of faith. An attempt was made to save the normative claim of the Gospel message for the present age by separating out and relativising entire complexes of textual content. But as the Gospel lost its alien and incomprehensible aspects in the process, at the same time it was adapted and changed to accord with present-day structures of understanding and experience.

Yet objectifying and aestheticising procedures attach to the entire contradictory and stratified body of the text. They afford a new readiness to understand the text: one which attributes validity to all statements and stories, but only intrinsically, as it were, and not in respect of the interpreter's world and behaviour. In the sense that past reports of and testimonies to miraculous events which are said to change reality in some way are subjected to scholarly research, they are indeed retained. At the same time, however, our distance from them is methodically confirmed. The interpretation of biblical texts as 'linguistic events', without questioning their reality beyond or chronologically before their communication, and the reduction of their truth to inner structures and relations, betray the character and alien nature of the texts, yet deprive them of all authority to interrogate present-day life and human behaviour.[7] The objectifying and aestheticising process attains to a kind of understanding, but one which implies a loss of validity and nomativity. The price paid for understanding is arbitrariness.

2. THE OPPRESSED AS AUTHORITIES IN THE RECEPTION OF THE MESSAGE

Hence the question arises whether there is a fundamental hermeneutical method which neither subjects the texts to contemporary dominant modes of understanding, adapting them inauthentically thereto, nor arbitrarily relegates them to the background, where they remain uncomprehended. The question is whether there are individuals in civil society who do not have to play off validity and incomprehensibly of contents against one another. For those who enjoy no actual power and autonomy in civil society, the hermeneutical question is posed somewhat differently: powerlessness, poverty and oppression are characteristic of people in highly-developed industrial societies whose specific value in respect of the hermeneutical question is something quite different to power and autonomy. Powerlessness, poverty and oppression characterise people in regard to the interpretation of Scripture, not from the standpoint of what they possess, or from that of what they are intrinsically, but from that of what they do not have and are not, and of what is done to them.[8]

The justification of poverty, powerlessness and oppression by recourse to Scripture cannot be the concern of those who are subjected to those things, but only the interest of those who dominate them and obtain some advantage from such circumstances. To that extent, the poor have nothing to read into the biblical texts other than their hope of and openness to receiving something from that source. Those without power are not therefore in a situation to establish by themselves a relationship to the good news in accordance with their criteria and their precedents, but must refer to unbroken tradition. Powerlessness is characteristic of those strategies which make them seem incapable of abrogating, modifying or wholly reconstituting traditions.

Powerlessness implies this 'ability' to let traditions apply intrinsically. The poor and oppressed are those for whom the texts and their contents can most readily win validity and response. For they believe in Jesus Christ not because they wish to remain poor, but so that they may be redeemed and liberated from want and distress. Only a group of people characterised thus has no superiority in regard to the good news. Therefore their recourse to elements of tradition does not harbour a danger of falsification. In poverty the kingdom of God cannot be identified with this life; in poverty all that can be conceived is that is must be endured. Therefore poverty is provocation and a reason for hope of liberation. Because those who are impoverished have every reason to hope in God, they have authority in their longing for liberation and redemption; they are authorities on faith.

It is impossible 'to understand the Christian God without the poor, without the defenceless, without the despised: in short, without the needy. A God separated from the poor may be anything but the God of revelation'.[9]

This characterisation of the privileged hearers of the word is not a general pronouncement about the status of a philosophy of the subject or an abstract anthropology (one devoid of individuals); it is a specific characteristic of a group or class of human beings. That is, poverty and powerlessness are not characteristics which appertain to people by virtue of their human nature or because of natural conditions; they are products of human activity. To that extent, the poor and powerless referred to here are those deprived by social structures and activities of the possibilities of self-realisation, material provisions, and a certain standard of living. Poverty and powerlessness are made. They do not come about without the power and interest of those who are neither impoverished nor weak.

As specific characteristics of human beings, these terms are theological precisely because they imply the question of guilt and causation.

Yet the antithesis of poverty and guilt, and identification as the sole guilty ones of those who have the social power; of, that is, those who possess power in relation to the powerless, seems far too simple. Surely the poor and powerless are at least jointly guilty for their inadequacies?

Some light may be thrown on this question of co-responsibility if we assume the existence of an anthropological, historical and philosophical nexus. If we suppose society to be in a state of development and that every person is endowed with the ability and energy also by his or her own efforts to develop his or her human existence and future happiness, then there is at least the possibility of co-responsibility in having neglected the struggle against poverty or in having waged it inappropriately. If, however, such evolutionary notions are theologically obsolete, then the idea of joint guilt must also disappear. Nevertheless, we should not underestimate the phenomenon observable especially in western industrial societies of the less well-off ruling class standards as their yardstick, and avoiding both a realistic assessment of their situation and thereby inhibiting the exercise of solidarity. That is to say, the identification of the powerful and of those responsible for social conditions as guilty does not imply an *a priori* lack of guilt on the part of those without power. The guilt of the powerless may lie precisely in an orientation to the norms and values of the powerful who are essentially guilty. But any further statements in this regard require more exact and refined analyses.

In theological discussion about who the socially identifiable authorities responding to the Gospel may be, the poor and powerless are poor and powerless primarily because of guilty human beings. Yet they only become meaningful reference values for theology and for exegesis and proclamation of the Gospel, if their situation is something that already exists for the Church as a community of faith. Their situation cannot be the product of ecclesiastical activity—of, say, some pastoral action, to cite an example in which the longing for redemption and the capacity to hear the Gospel are not obscured by power and riches. If human poverty and powerlessness in the world were produced by Church action, then it would be cynical to cite the poor and powerless as privileged hearers of the world. The proverbial saying 'Need teaches us to pray' is true, but only because it is prescribed for the Church. Pious meditation and prayer do anything but ask for a state of need, and to inculcate prayer by artificially inducing want would be the ultimate falsehood.

The theological concept of poverty and oppression implies an inquiry into their social origins; it also implies their objectivity and, as it were, their prescription for the Church's task of proclamation. Hence the value and theological necessity of the evangelical counsel of poverty for religious orders. Consequently the voluntary testimony of religious poverty is a witness of faith, an essential aspect of practical religion, inasmuch as the radical existential solidarity of Christians with, and their closeness to, the poor equip them to hear the Word.

In pre-industrial societies poverty was a state in which it was possible to live, even though miserably. For most people in the far too wide margins of capitalist welfare societies poverty and oppression represent a mortal threat. Poverty is not a condition of life which is only quantitatively different from that of the rich; for many people it is a condition of death. For those menaced by poverty there is no question of a choice between remaining poor or becoming rich. If they want to live or to survive, the poor have to do something to combat their poverty. The removal of universal poverty, hunger and want is not something that can be postponed. It puts those who believe that all people are intended to enjoy life in its fulness under pressure to act, and to act soon.

3. THE TRADITION OF THE OPPRESSED

Those who are not sufficiently powerful to built their own world from which they can profit, and to embellish it with appropriate ideas, have another way of relating to the past, even though they live under the conditions of a world controlled and constituted along bourgeois lines. Of course their 'powerless' relation to history does not allow them to prescribe the conditions for knowledge of past events and individuals. Instead they must have recourse to traditions which enable them to find some sort of direction in their struggle against their own death.[10]

This dependence on the past and on the tradition of struggle against oppression and poverty offers a form of reference to the past which escapes the deformations caused by domination. Instead the way in which the poor relate to their own traditions and to the word of God shows them that the modes of knowledge and perception practised by their social rulers tend to replicate and to project their rule back into history. An obvious aspect of this procedure is a selective approach to what has actually happened in history. It is the history of the top individuals—of the victors—which has been and continues to be written down. Further study of the social nature of historical sources would uncover many examples of this tendency.[11]

Nevertheless the history of conquerors which present-day rulers use in order to perceive only their counterparts in the past, and thus to confirm their own power, is not to be identified with tradition. Emancipation from the past and from authority and tradition is an essential part of bourgeois domination. Autonomous citizens confident of their own exercise of reason and practical competence no longer have to secure their rule by legitimising it by recourse to tradition. They do not rule because the oppressed believe that their rulers are the true successors to rulers of the past,[12] but merely because they themselves have produced and monopolised the material means (money and technology) for the exercise of power.

This kind of reference to the past is obvious in historicism. The past becomes the object of consideration and is thus deprived of its effect on the present. The objectification of the past does on the one hand concede that the dead are dead, but it also effaces any reminiscent protest against being dead and against closing the past off. The secret goal of rule in highly-industrialised and capitalist class societies may be said to consist in making people cogs in a vast piece of machinery, and in reducing them to their function and utility in the social whole. In this way, capitalism tends to efface the condition of subjectivity, and domination culminates in an objectification of dead people—people of the past. Their mortality is finally sealed by the effacement of any relation to the past; of, that is, any relation which (though without denying their death) even acknowledges that the dead are in any way significant as far as present-day activity is concerned and thus recognises a form of relation to them. It is probable that only thus, in regard to their authority for contemporary struggles, can hope for the dead be maintained.[13]

If we agree that the oppressed and poor of a society have another form of association with the past which may be roughly described as dependence on the relation to past events and individuals, then that tradition of the oppressed is the continuum of tradition of faith and hope. It is a continnum whose guarantors are intrinsically without hope and futureless in their own regard. The preservation of tradition then amounts to something more than the theory and practice of current historical research; that kind of tradition of the oppressed always miscarries, and indeed is turned upside down if purely objectifying methods are used. Then suffering and struggle receive mere scholarly recognition and become just another part of the cultural heritage. As much, the documentation of past defeats can yet again destroy the hope of the oppressed, for if this tradition is known in a purely objective way it is abrogated as a force capable of producing and directing current praxis.

Therefore the tradition of the oppressed does not persist universally and for everyone, but only for the currently poor and desperate and only where they suffer—only in their proximity. To stand in the tradition of the oppressed, in the continuum of tradition of hope against oppression, is still not identical with liberation from despair and impasse, but their most extreme refinement. The humble and believing reception of this tradition occurs in the only place where it is possible, one which is still endangered and threatened—as threatened as the oppressed themselves.

If faith in and remembrance of God's saving action in history are socially located, and the authorities for that faith are describable in terms of the tradition of the oppressed, then we must ask whether this is more than a mere hermeneutical construction. Surely the poor and oppressed are those least fitted to receive the good news? Surely their social condition as those who suffer understandably inclines them to believe any false promise and to accept fantasies? That this is a serious objection is clear from the nature of the popular press and literature and the type of person who reads them. I have already referred to the fact that the socially marginalised an oppressed often adopt the values and norms of the better-off and powerful. Such questions force us to move beyond the political and economic aspects of a theological hermeneutics to the cultural plane. The questions of the consciousness, values and ideas of the oppressed cannot be explained merely in terms of material and economic oppression. Precisely because of material oppression those affected by it are also open to oppression in the areas of culture and consciousness. There is a danger that they will produce no ideas of their own which are appropriate to their situation, together with associated realistic wishes and needs, but that they will use the concepts which others, namely richer and more powerful people, have produced for their own purposes. A central aspect of the bourgeois notion of self is a consciousness of one's own potentialities and capacities for shaping one's own life and so on. If someone takes up this claim to the autonomy and apples it to himself or herself, but is without the appropriate material means to go further, frictions and contradictions result. The consequence is, first, an illusionary falsification of the experienced reality of oppression and, second, behaviour which forces the marginalised even deeper into debt, poverty and dependence.

But the proposition that the poor and oppressed are the authorities for hearing of the word does not imply that they always and inevitably exercise this authority which they possess. Obviously, in Europe at least, there is a level of oppression which affects values, norms, consciousness of reality and modes of perception. To that extent the poor are not an empty barrel into which the Gospel can be most easily poured. That is possible only if the poor perceive their situation realistically, with an inclination to identify with the culture and values of the oppressors. Heeding the Gospel is oppressed to that form of bourgeois socialisation on the basis of which the really poor fall into debt, become avid consumers, make their happiness dependent on status symbols, and are driven into isolation (because, for instance, of the tabus attaching to financial problems).

A second objection to the tradition of the oppressed as the essential concept of a theological hermeneutics would be the possibility of that reducing the Gospel to a kind of fideism. Is any non-objectifying reference to the past at all credible? Perhaps recourse to the tradition of hope and dependence on tradition are a form of conditioning of faith which makes it indistinguishable from mere suppostion? A consciousness of and an orientation to socially transformative praxis which arise from dependence on tradition do not seem to accord with truth. We are brought full circle when dependence on tradition becomes the criterion whether the truth and credibility of that tradition can be demonstrated.

The charge of fideism and of an implicit circularity in the thesis that the oppressed are authorities in hearing the liberating Gospel would be justified if poverty and faith were synonymous. If one had only to be poor to be a Christian then poverty would produce, so to speak, a politico-economically ordained anonymous Christendom.

We have to make a distinction here. Anyone who is poor is not 'a believer' by sole virtue of that poverty. Anyone who is poor is a privileged, specially summoned, selected hearer and recipient of the Gospel. On account of their poverty the poor have most reason for faith and objectively the most poignant longing for redemption. Because God has founded their hope in despite of their social situation, they are authorities in the matter of faith. That is also the reason why we cannot speak in exactly the same way of all poor people all over the world. The historical situation reveals considerable differences between many poor and disadvantaged people in the highly-developed countries, especially in English-speaking and German-language areas, and especially in Latin america.

The traditional truth of the oppressed is not conterminous with their oppression but consists in the realistic assessment of that oppression and in its faithful rejection. To that extent, the tradition of the oppressed as the key notion of a theological hermeneutic does not lead to a fideistic circularity. Their situation makes the poor, powerless and oppressed especially capable of hearing the word, and of interpreting Scripture and the texts of Tradition. Whether faith and hope actually reach through to people in this situation and take effect in the practice of resistance, remains the work of grace and unassignable; it is something that can be related only subsequently but cannot be deduced by sheer force of argument.[15]

Translated by J. G. Cumming

Notes

1. On the difference from bourgeois freedom and autonomy of the Christian notion of freedom, see J. B. Metz 'Wider die zweite Unmündigkeit' in: J. Rusen *et al* (eds), *Die Zukunft der Aufklarung* (Frankfurt 1968).

2. See the interesting contribution by Werner Muller 'Bürgertum und Christentum' in *Christlicher Glaube in moderner Gesellschaft* Enzykloädische Bibliotek (ed. von F. Böckle, F. X. Kaufmann, K. Rahner, B. Welte) vol. 18 49.

3. *Ibid.* 39

4. C. Hartlich 'Is the Historico-Critical Method out-of-date?' in *Concilium* (1980) 536.

5. A new understanding of the historicity of biblical texts rejects this kind of selective tendency in historico-critical methodology. The events which are described in the biblical texts, even if they cannot be understood today just as they are, have authority and validity because their actual existence cannot simply be denied. This kind of confirmation of the historicity of biblical events in spite of their incompatibility with typical present-day experience ensures reminiscent and narrative recourse to the two testaments.

6. Cf., in this regard F. X. Kaufmann and T B Metz, *Zukunftsfähigkeit. Suchbewegungen im Christentum* (Freiburg 1987) 117ff.

7. 'Inasmuch as the phenomenon becomes an object, the effect or significance which it exerts on me or has for me is effaced.' R. Bultmann *Wissenschaft und Existenz* in *id.*, *Glauben und Verstehen* III (Tübingen 1960) 108.

8. Cf., W. Kern and C. Link 'Autonomie und Geschöpflinchkeit' in *Christlicher Glaube in moderner Gesellschaft* Enzyklopädische Bibliotek (ed. von F. Böckle, F. X. Kaufmann, K. Rahner, B. Welte) Vol. 18 (Freiburg 1982) 131. What Link sees as a universal anthropological proposition about the doctrine of justification may be used to describe this hermeneutical approach.

9. C. Boff and J. Pixley *Die Option fur die Armen* (Düsseldorf 1987) 126.

10. Trying to explain the significance of the defeat which Fascism had prepared for the oppressed class, Benjamin saw the remembrance of the history of suffering of the oppressed as the last possibility of maintaining the claim to liberation. Only a class which is directed 'more by the true image of enslaved predecessors than by the ideal image of liberated descendants' (W. Benjamin *Gesammelte Schriften* Vol. 1 [Frankfurt 1974] 1237) can resist Fascism. Hence under Fascist oppression historical materialism came close to theology. Cf., in this regard W. Benjamin 'Über den Begriff der Geschichte' in *id.*, *Gesammelte Schriften* Vol. 1 (Frankfurt 1974) 691ff.

11. Cf., O. John '. . . and this enemy has not ceased to prevail'. *Die Bedeutung W. Benjamins für eine Theologie nach Auschwitz*. Münster diss. (1982) 512–39.

12. Cf., *ibid.*, 180ff.

13. 'Unsere Hoffnung. Ein Bekenntnis zum Glauben in dieser Zeit' in *Gemeinsame Synode der Bistümer in der Bundesrepublik Deutschland*. Official ed. (Ed. for German Bishops' Conference) (Freiburg 1976) 91.

14. On this basis it is possible to see the self-understanding of theology as an *actus secundus*, dependent on a precedent faith praxis of the Church.

15. There are many reports on the faith of the oppressed people of Latin America. See C. Mesters 'Understanding of Scripture in some Brazilian Basic Communities' in *Concilium* (1980).

Contributors

ADELA YARBRO COLLINS is Professor of New Testament at the University of Notre Dame. Publications include *The Combat Myth in the Book of Revelation* (1976); *The Apocalypse: A Biblical and Theological Commentary* (1979); *Crisis and Catharsis: The Power of the Apocalypse* (1984); and articles in the *Harvard Theological Review*, the *Catholic Bible Quarterly*, and the *Journal of Biblical Literature*. She is editor of the Society of Biblical Literature Monograph Series and a member of the Executive Committee of the Catholic Biblical Association.

ENRIQUE DUSSEL'S academic background includes a licentiateship in philosophy (Mendoza), a doctorate in philosophy (Madrid) and in history (The Sorbonne), a licentiateship in theology (Paris) and in 1981 a doctorate in theology *honoris causa* (Fribourg). Currently he is Professor of Church History and Theology (ITES, Mexico) and of Ethics and Political Philosophy (UNAM, Mexico). He is president of CEHILA and co-ordinator of *The Working Commission for Church History* and a member of the Executive Committee (IAMS). Recent publications include *History of the Church of Latin America* (1981), *Philosophy of Liberation* (New York 1985); a *General Introduction* to *Historia General de la Iglesia en América Latina* (1983); *Hacia un Marx desconocido. Comentario a los manuscritos del 61–63* (*SIGLO XXI*) (1988; *Caminhos de libertação latino-americana* (*PAULINOS*) (1985); *Para una historia de la teología en América Latina* (1985) and in the *Teología y Liberación* series, *Etica comunitaria* (1986; English edition 1988).

MICHAEL ERBE was born in 1940 in Berlin, studied history and classical philology at the Free University of Berlin where he gained his doctorate and post-doctoral qualification also there in 1974. In 1975 he was appointed Professor for European History of the Early Modern Age at the Free

University Berlin. Since 1985 he has been its First Vice-President. Relevant publications include: *Studien zur Entwicklung des Niederkirchenwesens in Ostsachsen vom 8. bis zum 12.Jahrhundert* (Göttingen 1969); (ed.) *Quellen zur germanischen Bekehrungsgeschichte (5.-8.Jahrhundert)* (Gütersloh 1971); *Pfarrkirche und Dorf. Ausgewählte Quellen zur Geschichte des Niederkirchenwesens in Nordwest- und Mittel-deutschland vom 8. bis zum 16. Jahrhundert* (Gütersloh 1973); since 1981 he has been co-editor of the *Archivs für Reformationsgeschichte*.

SEAN FREYNE is currently Professor of Theology at Trinity College, Dublin, having previously lectured on Biblical Studies in the USA and Australia. His theological and biblical studies were completed at St Patrick's College, Maynooth, Ireland, the Biblical Institute, Rome, and the *Institutum Judaicum* of the University of Tübingen, West Germany. He is the author of a number of books and articles on Second Temple Judaism and Early Christianity, most recently *Galilee, Jesus and the Gospels. Literary Approaches and Historical Investigations* (1988). He joined the editorial board of *Concilium* in 1987 and is also currently on the editorial board of *New Testament Studies*.

GIOVANNI GONNET. Born in Geneva in 1909, the author studied at the University or Rome where he obtained, in 1952, the title of privat-docent in the history of Christianity. Course supervisor at the Waldensian Faculty of Theology in Rome from 1950, he taught successively at the Universities of Oslo, Bari and Cosenza. From the time of his degree thesis (*Il Valdismo medioevale. Prolegomeni*, 1942), he has been especially interested in the historiography relating to religious 'dissent' from the 12th to the 16th century. His publications include: *Bibliografia Valdese*, in collaboration with A. Armand-Hugon (1953); *Enchiridion Fontium Valdensium* (1958); *Le confessioni di fede valdesi prima della Riforma* (1967); *Les Vaudois au Moyen Age*, in collaboration with A. Molnar, (1974); and *Le eresie e i movimenti popolari del Basso Medioevo* (1976).

EUGÈNE HONÉE was born in 1934. He studied philosophy and history at Nijmegen, Church history at Rome (Nederlands Historisch Instituut) and Mainz (Institut für europäische Geschichte). Since 1982 he has been professor of Church history at the Theological University of Amsterdam. Together with E. Kerstiens he published a Dutch adaptation with commentary of M. Merleau-Ponty's *Éloge de la Philosophie* (1979). His publications in the field of Church history have been particularly concerned with the Reformation: *Studien zum Augsburger Reichstag* (1973); *Over de opzet en mislukking van een godsdienstgesprek. Het 'Konvent' van Hagenau* (1982); *Der Libell des Hieronymus Vehus zum Augsburger Reichstag 1530. Untersuchung und Texte zur katholischen Concordia-Politik* (1988).

OTTMAR JOHN was born at Herford, Westphalia, in 1953. He graduated in theology at Münster in 1983 and received an MPhil at the same university in 1985. He is a research assistant in the fundamental theological section at Münster.

HANS-WINFRIED JÜNGLING, born 1938, is a member of the Society of Jesus and Professor of Old Testament Exegesis at the Philosophical-Theological College of St George, Frankfurt am Main, West Germany. His publications include: *Richter 19—Ein Plädoyer für das Königtum. Stilistische Analyse der Tendenzerzählung Ri 19,1–30a; 21,25* (Rome 1981); *Ich bin Gott—keiner sonst. Annäherung an das Alte Testament* (Würzburg 1981/Leipzig 1986); '"Auge für Auge, Zahn für Zahn." Bemerkungen zu Sinn und Geltung der alttestamentlichen Talionsformeln' *Theologie und Philosophie* 59 (1984) 1–38.

HANS-JOSEF KLAUCK was born 1946 in Hermeskeil near Trier in West Germany. He is Franciscan and was ordained priest in Münster in 1973. Since 1982 he has been professor of New Testament exegesis at the Catholic Faculty of Theology at the University of Würzburg. His publications include: *Allegorie und Allegorese in synoptischen Gleichnistexten* 1978,² 1986; *Hausgemeinde und Hauskirche im frühen Christentum* 1981; *Herrenmahl und hellenistischer Kult* 1982, ²1986; *1. Korintherbrief* 1984, ²1987; *Brot vom Himmel* 1985; *2. Korintherbrief* 1986, ²1988; and *Judas—ein Jünger des Herrn*, 1987.

JONATHAN MAGONET has a first degree in medicine, received Rabbinic ordination from Leo Baeck College, London and obtained his PhD from the University of Heidelberg for a thesis on the Book of Jonah, subsequently published as 'Form and Meaning: Studies in Literary Techniques in the Book of Jonah.' He was recently appointed Principal of Leo Baeck College after ten years as Head of the Department of Bible Studies. He has co-edited with Rabbi Lionel Blue two prayerbooks for the Reform Synagogues of Great Britain (Forms of Prayer: Vol I, Daily and Sabbath; Vol II, Days of Awe). For almost twenty years he has organised an annual Jewish-Christian Bible Week and, for twelve, a Jewish-Christian-Muslim Student Conference at the Hedwig Dransfeld Haus in West Germany.

HERMAN OBDEIJN was born in 1938 and studied philosophy and theology in Leuven and Carthage, and history at the Catholic University of Nijmegen. In 1975 he obtained his doctorate with a thesis on the theme of the teaching of history in modern Tunisia, 1881–1970. From 1970 to 1975 he worked on development projects in Tunisia; from 1976 to 1982 he was on the staff of the Catholic University of Nijmegen; and from 1982 to 1985 was cultural attaché to the Dutch embassy in Rabat. Since 1985 he has been co-ordinator of minority studies at the Rijksuniversiteit in Leiden. His publications include *The Political Role of Catholic and Protestant Missions in the Colonial Partition of Black Africa. A Bibliographical Essay* Intercontinenta 3 (Leiden 1983); 'De Witte Paters en de christelijke omwenteling in Buganda in het laatste kwart van de 19e eeuw' in J. M. Schoffeleers ed. *Missie en Ontwikkeling in Oost-Afrika* (Nijmegen en Baarn 1983) 40–53; 'Les Soeurs Blanches en Afrique centrale à la fin du XIXe siècle. Les idées, le personnel, les oeuvres' *La femme dans les sociétés coloniales* (Aix-en-Provence 1984) 192–202; and a bibliographical intro-duction to Africa mission, 'Missie en Zending in Afrika. Een bibliografische inleiding' in *Tijdschrift voor Geschiedenis* 98 (1985) 381–392.

MARJORIE E. REEVES has been Tutor, then Fellow and Vice-Principal of St Anne's College, Oxford and University Lecturer, 1939–1972. She is a Fellow of the Royal Historical Society of the British Academy and is a Corresponding Fellow of the Medieval Academy of America. Publications include: (with L. Tondelli and B. Hirsch-Reich) *Il Libro delle figure dell' Abate Gioachino da Fiore* (Turin 1953); *The Influence of Prophecy in the Later Middle Ages* (Oxford 1969); (with B. Hirsch-Reich) *The Figurae of Joachim of Fiore* (Oxford 1972); (with W. Gould) *Joachim of Fiore and the Myth of the Eternal Evangel in the Nineteenth Century* (Oxford 1987).

BERNARD RENAUD was born in 1929 in Angers and is a priest. He studied theology in Angers and Rome (St Thomas University) and did his biblical studies at the Pontifical Institute in Rome and the French Biblical and Archeological School in Jerusalem. From 1960 to 1972, he taught Old Testament exegesis at Angers. Since 1972 he has been professor of Old Testament exegesis at the Catholic Theology Faculty in Strasbourg.

He has contributed to numerous journals including *La Revue biblique, Biblica, Vetus Testmentum, Zeitschrift für die alttestamentliche Wissenschaft,* and *La Revue des Sciences Religieuses*. His publications include: *Je suis un Dieu Jaloux* (1963), *Structure et attaches littéraires de Michée IV–V* (1964); *La Formation du livre de Michée* (Etudes Bibliques 1977); a commentary on *Michée, Sophonie, Nahum* (Sources bibliques 1987).

CHRISTOPHER ROWLAND, born in Doncaster, England in 1947. He studied theology at Cambridge University and, after five years lecturing at the University of Newcastle upon Tyne, returned there as Dean of Jesus College and is now also University Lecturer in New Testament Studies. He is a member of the Board of Christian Aid, the Development Agency of the British Council of Churches and chairs its Latin American and Caribbean Committee. He is married with four children and is a priest of the Church of England. He has written on Jewish apocalyptic, Christian origins, and radical movements in the Christian church.

ANTON WEILER was born at Voorburg, the Netherlands, in 1927. He read philosophy and history at Nijmegen University. Since 1964 he has been professor of general and Dutch medieval history, and since 1965 professor of the philosophy of history, at the Catholic University of Nijmegen. Since 1984 he has been principal of the Catholic Theological College at Utrecht. He has published articles and the following books: *Heinrich von Gorkum (1431). Seine Stellung in der Philosophie und in der Theologie des Spätmittelalters* (Hilversum and Einsiedeln (1962); *Geschiedenis van de kerk in Nederland* (Utrecht 1963) (with de Jong, Rogier and Monnich); *Deus in terris. Middeleeuwse wortels vaan de totalitaire ideologie* (Hilversum 1965); *Necrologie, Kroniek en cartularium c.a. van het fraterhuis te Doesburg* (1432–1559) (Leiden 1974); *Christelijk bestaan in een seculaire cultuur* (Roermond 1969) (with others); *Monasticon Windeshememse, Part 3: The Netherlands* (Brussels 1980) (with Noel Geirnaert).

RECENTLY PUBLISHED

Galilee, Jesus and the Gospels
Literary Approaches and Historical Investigations
SEAN FREYNE

In this original and methodologically concerned contribution to modern gospel studies, the author shows how the particularity of Jesus' Galilean origins is both historically important and theologically relevant. He takes the Galilean context of Jesus' life and subjects it to close analysis, integrating questions of social identity and theological reflection. **£10.95**

Text and Interpretation
As Categories of Theological Thinking
WERNER G. JEANROND

'A book of high quality, combining intelligent thinking with understandable style. . .' *Hans Küng* **£12.95**

The Truth in Love
Reflections on Christian Morality
VINCENT MacNAMARA

The author's concern is to promote a critical and credible morality; those who read and reflect on this book will agree that he succeeds brilliantly. **£7.95**

Creation and Redemption
GABRIEL DALY, O.S.A.

Envisages creation and redemption not as two separate acts in the divine-human drama, but as one continuous unfolding of God's creative purposes. **£7.95**

A Pilgrim God for a Pilgrim People
DENIS CARROLL

The idea of God is unacceptable to many; to others it is irrelevant to their daily concerns. The author argues that this situation can provide a unique opportunity for growth in a living faith. **£7.95**

GILL & MACMILLAN

CONCILIUM

CONCILIUM

CONCILIUM 1987

All back issues are still in print: available from bookshops (price £5.45) or direct from the publishers (£5.95/US$9.95/Can$11.75 including postage and packing).

T & T CLARK LTD, 59 GEORGE STREET EDINBURGH EH2 2LQ, SCOTLAND

SUBSCRIBE TO CONCILIUM

'CONCILIUM a journal of world standing, is far and away the best.'

The Times

'... it is certainly the most variegated and stimulating school of theology active today. **CONCILIUM** ought to be available to all clergy and layfolk who are anxious to keep abreast of what is going on in the theological workshops of the world today.'

Theology

CONCILIUM is published on the first of every alternate month beginning in February. Over twelve issues (two years), themes are drawn from the following key areas: dogma, liturgy, pastoral theology, ecumenism, moral theology, the sociology of religion, Church history, canon law, spirituality, scripture, Third World theology and Feminist theology (see back cover for details of 1988 titles). As a single issue sells for £5.45 a subscription can mean savings of up to £12.75.

SUBSCRIPTION RATES 1988

	UK	USA	Canada	Other Countries
New Subscribers	£19.95	$39.95	$49.95	£19.95
Regular Subscribers	£27.50	$49.95	$59.95	£27.50
Airmail		$65.00	$79.95	£37.50

All prices include postage and packing. **CONCILIUM** is sent 'accelerated surface post' to the USA and Canada and by surface mail to other destinations.

Cheques payable to T & T Clark. Personal cheques in $ currency acceptable. Credit card payments by *Access*, *Mastercard* and *Visa*.

'A bold and confident venture in contemporary theology. All the best new theologians are contributing to this collective summa'.

Commonweal

Send your order direct to the Publishers

T & T CLARK LTD

59 GEORGE STREET
EDINBURGH
EH2 2LQ
SCOTLAND

Publishers   *since 1821*